Facilitator's Guide to
GROUPWORK IN DIVERSE CLA...
A CASEBOOK FOR EDUCATOR...

Editors

Judith H. Shulman
WestEd

Rachel A. Lotan
Stanford University

Jennifer A. Whitcomb
University of Denver

Published by Teachers College Press, 1234 Amsterdam Avenue, New York, NY 10027

Library of Congress Cataloging-in-Publication Data

Facilitator's guide to Groupwork in diverse classrooms: a casebook for educators/
  Judith H. Shulman, Rachel A. Lotan, Jennifer A. Whitcomb.
     p.   cm.
   Companion vol. to Groupwork in diverse classrooms.
   Includes bibliographical references.
   ISBN 0-8077-3702-X (alk. paper)
   1. Group work in education—United States—Case studies.
   2. Socially handicapped children—Education—United States—Case studies.
   3. Case method (Education) I. Lotan, Rachel A. II. Whitcomb, Jennifer A.
   III. Groupwork in diverse classrooms. IV. Title.
   LB1032.S48 1998
   371.39'5—dc21   97-33506

Printed on acid-free paper
Manufactured in the United States of America

05 04 03 02 01 00 99 98   8 7 6 5 4 3 2 1

FACILITATOR'S GUIDE TO
GROUPWORK IN DIVERSE CLASSROOMS:
A CASEBOOK FOR EDUCATORS

Editors

JUDITH H. SHULMAN
WestEd

RACHEL A. LOTAN
Stanford University

JENNIFER A. WHITCOMB
University of Denver

TEACHERS COLLEGE PRESS

Teachers College, Columbia University
New York and London

TABLE OF CONTENTS

ACKNOWLEDGMENTS

Several people devoted considerable time and energy to this project. We are especially indebted to WestEd colleague Nikola Filby, who was a member of the advisory board, participated in the field test, wrote two of the teaching notes in this volume, and contributed her insights and wisdom in several critical meetings throughout the project.

Thanks also to our collaborators in the field test who spent several Saturdays participating in meetings at Stanford University, conducted case discussions at their sites, collected data, and provided invaluable input into the cases and discussion process. They include Joan Benton, California International Studies Program, Stanford University; Tuckie Yirchott, Bay Area Global Education Project, Stanford University; Joan Cunnings, Los Cerros Middle School, San Ramon School District; Janie Roskelley, Sally Scholl, and Pat Visher, Sycamore Valley Elementary School, San Ramon School District; Micaela Munoz and Donna Parrish, Tempe Elementary School District; Susan Schultz (who also contributed two cases), Menlo-Atherton High School, Sequoia Union School District; and Susana Mata, School of Education, Human Development and Educational Technology, California State University, Fresno.

We would also like to thank our administrative assistant, Rosemary De La Torre, who patiently kept us organized through several drafts of this text, and editors Sally Ianiro, Sarah Biondello, and Carol Collins, whose meticulous attention helped to make each sentence speak clearly.

Judith H. Shulman
Rachel A. Lotan
Jennifer A. Whitcomb

INTRODUCTION

This guide is a companion volume to *Groupwork in Diverse Classrooms: A Casebook for Educators*, which presents 16 cases designed to help individuals and groups analyze how to use groupwork effectively. Specifically, the guide offers the information needed to use these cases in structured professional development experiences.

Teacher-written cases, depicting real-life problems other teachers are likely to face, can be powerful tools for reflection on practice. They can help teachers anticipate problems and solutions as they learn from others' real-life stories. When read alone, they offer the reader the vicarious experience of walking in another's shoes. But in group discussion they are especially powerful, enabling differing points of view to be aired and examined.

During the last decade, educators have viewed case-based teaching as one of the most promising ways to reform teacher education and staff development (Sykes & Bird, 1992; J. Shulman, 1992). Staff at WestEd (formerly Far West Laboratory) have been active participants in this reform effort, developing casebooks, leading case discussions, conducting facilitator seminars, and coordinating national conferences. Our experience and research suggest case discussions can help participants bridge theory and practice, spot issues and frame problems in ambiguous situations, interpret situations from multiple perspectives, identify crucial decision points and possibilities for action, recognize potential risks and benefits inherent in any course of action, and identify and test teaching principles in real classroom situations. In short, cases and case discussions can help teachers develop flexibly powerful pedagogical understanding and judgment (L. Shulman, 1996).

But we also know the pitfalls of poor discussions. It is possible, for example, to participate in an animated case discussion and not learn. In our consultations with faculty who were learning to use the cases in our diversity casebook (J. Shulman & Mesa-Bains, 1993), we discovered that participation in discussions confirmed rather than diminished some teachers' tendencies toward racial stereotyping (J. Shulman, 1996).

Many educators have written cogently about how to lead case discussions (see, for example, Barnett, Goldenstein, & Jackson, 1994; Christensen, Garvin, & Sweet, 1991; Mesa-Bains & Shulman, 1994; Silverman, Welty, & Lyon, 1992; and Wassermann, 1994, 1995). This guide is directed specifically at enhancing analytic opportunities for the cases in the accompanying volume. Our experience suggests that the more knowledgeable a facilitator is about the issues in a case and the more she can anticipate the variety of participant responses in a case discussion, the greater the likelihood learning will occur as a result of the discussion.

Ultimately, knowledge gained from cases can provide inspiration and provocation to change teaching behaviors. Teachers typically lack the time and opportunity to reflect on their own and others' experience. In their day-to-day life in the classroom, they are usually confronted with a seamless continuum of experience from which they can think about individual kids as cases, or lessons as cases, but rarely do they coordinate the different dimensions into meaningful "chunks" (L. Shulman, 1996):

> Case methods thus become strategies for helping teachers to "chunk" their experience into units that can become the focus for reflective practice. They therefore can become the basis for individual teacher learning as well as a form within which communities of teachers, both local and extended, as members of visible and invisible colleges, can store, exchange and organize their experience. (p. 194)

ABOUT THIS VOLUME

Though groupwork among students of diverse backgrounds is recommended in most current reforms of teaching, we know that using it effectively is often complex and difficult to achieve. *Groupwork in Diverse Classrooms* addresses many of the typical dilemmas teachers face in their classrooms. Its teacher–authors describe in vivid detail their own successes and failures as they struggle with the complexities of teaching. Their compelling stories are excellent discussion catalysts offering others the rare opportunity to analyze from a safe distance situations they too face. Cases present abstract issues in concrete terms which mirror teachers' own experiences. Case discussion can lead teachers to examine their views, prejudices, and attitudes toward typical dilemmas on groupwork in their classrooms, and as a result, begin to seek and use new teaching strategies.

Each case provides the reader an opportunity to examine a number of issues as they occur in the real world of teaching—interwoven into complex dilemmas and situations. The table at the end of this introduction provides easy reference for locating specific issues within each case and across cases. Issues addressed in this volume include:

- examining why and how to use groupwork effectively;

- designing group tasks that complement one another and demand contributions from all group members;

- developing appropriate assessments for group activities;

- analyzing the appropriate role of a teacher during group activities;

- exploring the purpose of student roles during group activities;

- exploring constructive teacher interventions during group process;

- crafting groups that support learning for all students;

- supporting students in cooperating and collaborating with one another;

- dealing with uncooperative individuals and groups of students;

- providing effective status interventions;

- exploring how to communicate with parents who may be critical of group projects; and

- examining professional development activities for adults.

Part I offers a general introduction to facilitation methods. Part II provides teaching notes for each case in *Groupwork in Diverse Classrooms* which incorporate analyses of the issues embedded in the narrative and sample discussion questions for a case discussion. Much of the information presented in the notes draws from a year-long field test of the cases with different groups of teachers. Facilitators will find sample questions in the "Questions and Answers" section helpful as they work through their personal analyses of each case. The questions are designed to be asked directly of case participants, though we encourage facilitators to develop their own questions as well.

Together, *Groupwork in Diverse Classrooms* and the *Facilitator's Guide* provide content and structure for valuable experiences in reflective teaching. Facilitators should study both volumes before working with a group of teachers and should allow ample time for group members to reflect on the cases and share personal experiences. The result can be a powerful experience in professional development.

REFERENCES

Barnett, C., Goldenstein, D., & Jackson, B. (1994). *Mathematics teaching cases: Fractions, decimals, ratios, and percents—Hard to teach and hard to learn?* Portsmouth, NH: Heinemann.

Christensen, C. R., Garvin, D. A., & Sweet, A. (Eds.). (1991). *Education for judgment: The artistry of discussion leadership.* Boston: Harvard Business School.

Mesa-Bains, A., & Shulman, J. H. (1994). *Facilitator's guide to diversity in the classroom: A casebook for teachers and teacher educators.* Hillsdale, NJ: Lawrence Erlbaum Associates.

Shulman, J. H. (Ed.). (1992). *Case methods in teacher education.* New York: Teachers College Press.

Shulman, J. H. (1996). Tender feelings, hidden thoughts: Confronting bias, innocence, and racism through case discussions. In J. Colbert, P. Desberg, & K. Trimble (Eds.), *The case for education: Contemporary approaches for using case methods* (pp. 137–158). Boston: Allyn & Bacon.

Shulman, J. H., & Mesa-Bains, A. (Eds.). (1993). *Diversity in the classroom: A casebook for teachers and teacher educators.* Hillsdale, NJ: Lawrence Erlbaum Associates.

Shulman, L. S. (1996). "Just in case": Reflections on learning from experience. In J. Colbert, P. Desberg, & K. Trimble (Eds.), *The case for education: Contemporary approaches for using case methods.* Boston: Allyn & Bacon.

Silverman, R., Welty, W. M., & Lyon, S. (1992). *Case studies for teacher problem solving.* New York: McGraw-Hill.

Sykes, G., & Bird, T. (1992). Teacher education and the case idea. In G. Grant (Ed.), *Review of research in education* (pp. 457–521). Washington, DC: American Educational Research Association.

Wassermann, S. (1994). *Introduction to case methods teaching.* New York: Teachers College Press.

Wassermann, S. (1995). *Serious players and primary schools.* New York: Teachers College Press.

Table 1

Overview of Issues Across Cases

Case No.	Purposes for groupwork	Design of groupwork tasks	Assessment	Role of the teacher	When and how to intervene	Crafting groups	Use of student roles	Supporting cooperation and collaboration	Uncooperative students/group/class	Status problems	Status interventions	Communication with parents and other teachers	Groupwork in professional development	English learners
Case 1	X			X	X			X		X				
Case 2	X	X	X											
Case 3	X	X				X	X		X					
Case 4	X	X	X	X	X		X	X	X					
Case 5	X	X	X									X		
Case 6	X	X		X	X	X		X		X	X			X
Case 7		X	X	X	X	X	X			X				
Case 8		X		X	X			X		X			X	
Case 9	X	X		X	X	X	X	X						
Case 10	X	X		X	X			X	X					
Case 11	X	X	X	X				X	X	X	X			
Case 12		X	X	X		X		X		X	X			
Case 13	X	X		X			X	X		X	X			X
Case 14	X	X	X									X		
Case 15		X				X		X		X		X	X	
Case 16	X	X	X	X	X		X	X	X	X	X			X

Table 1. Overview of Issues Across Cases

PART I: FACILITATING A CASE DISCUSSION

Preparation and Process

Much can be learned just by reading cases. But a good facilitator can expedite that learning by prompting a group to examine the case's issues in ways that readers by themselves might not. Far more than a lecture, case discussion enlivens content and helps participants internalize theory. Still, the idea of facilitating such discussion can be intimidating: when you don't do all the talking, you relinquish authority and therefore can't be entirely sure how the class is going to go.

This concern is heightened when the cases are problem focused—as all these cases are—and the authors are honest about the dilemmas they face in their classrooms, the surprises that occur, and the reflective questions they ask themselves about how they handled the situation. In the pilot test of *Groupwork in Diverse Classrooms*, teachers identified with authors as they struggled to cope with events. The stronger their identification with an author, the more vulnerable they often were during a case discussion because a criticism of the way the author handled a situation was considered a criticism of themselves.

CONSTRUCTING A CASE-BASED PROFESSIONAL DEVELOPMENT CURRICULUM

Ideally, case discussions don't take place in isolation; they are part of a case-based curriculum—a whole course or program built around the use of cases and including additional readings about the issues being addressed. Case discussion becomes more meaningful when supporting materials explain the general principles exemplified by the case. Conversely, the specific real people and situations detailed in each case add flesh and blood to otherwise nebulous concepts.

One of the problems in professional development workshops on groupwork is the tendency to provide prescriptions and "how-to"s without providing opportunities for teachers to link the prescriptions to analyses of specific classroom situations. Without analyses for people to work through, the learning that takes place is disembodied and therefore easily forgotten.

Cases, by contrast, can introduce an individual student, teacher, and classroom, bringing that world to life in all its complexity. Problems under discussion are no longer those of, say, low-status students, but of Dennis, Roberto, and Robert—very memorable, real young people with feelings, talents, and families. Their needs may or may not be typical, but their teachers try to meet them in the best ways they can. Teachers reading and discussing these cases can use the specific situation as a vehicle for questioning their own instructional practices, status interventions, and purposes for groupwork and for reflecting on their own values, attitudes, and experience. Ideally, information in the case is supplemented by other materials—for example, psychological and sociological readings on how to encourage low-status students and models of cooperative learning that offer specific strategies for handling such students. Because it provides complexity and a meaningful context, the case can function as the hub of the staff development wheel.

Though reading or discussing a single case can be beneficial, it is the sustained use of cases in group discussion that spurs classroom change. A group often needs to discuss at least four cases to acquire the comfort level, equity of participation, and analytical skills that allow discussion to move to more insightful levels. Moreover, the transfer of insights and knowledge to the classroom doesn't really happen until reflective practices are internalized. The educators who participated in the field test and members of the advisory board noted that by analyzing how similar dilemmas played out in a variety of cases, teachers are more likely to make sound judgments when faced with comparable situations in their classrooms.

For each curriculum, case selection should be customized. In preservice, where participants have not yet tested themselves in the day-to-day life of the classroom, a varied group of cases offering insights into the world they are about to enter will be helpful. Though teacher education students have been in classrooms as *students* for 16 years, they need to "make the familiar strange" and begin to analyze teaching from a *teacher's* perspective. Case discussions enable teacher educators to "complexify" day-to-day teaching situations and guide their students to develop the analytic skills required to make strategic judgments in their classrooms.

Student teachers who have used these cases have asserted their importance, especially those who had already done some practice teaching in the field. They reported that the cases "ring true," that they could identify with the problems in the case, and that it was comforting to know that skilled veterans were struggling with some of the same kinds of problems they were.

In the inservice environment, cases should have clear links to circumstances at participants' schools so that teachers can compare the case experiences with their own. For example, if a school has a number of limited English speaking students, "Struggles With the Dynamics of Grouping" and "The Chance I Had Been Waiting For" are likely candidates. The cases lead teachers to identify grouping strategies and appropriate status interventions to integrate limited English speaking students into classroom life.

Another means of enhancing the usefulness of the cases is asking participants to keep journals and jot down observations about the cases that draw on their classroom experiences. Journals become catalysts that move participants to begin writing up their own cases. Our research suggests there is a strong correlation between case writing and teacher learning.

An on-site, case-based professional development seminar can have schoolwide effects. Teacher isolation is reduced as participants discover the strength of group problem solving. Consequently, teachers may risk modifying the instruction in their classrooms. They may also apply group problem solving to other school issues, including deciding their own professional development needs.

PREPARING TO LEAD DISCUSSION

Careful preparation is critical to leading case discussions successfully. You'll need a thorough knowledge of the case as well as clear ideas about how best to use the teaching notes to guide the sessions.

Reading the case. To facilitate a discussion effectively, one cardinal rule applies: you must have a good grasp of the case and its nuances. This is true for any case, but it's especially crucial when delicate subject matter is involved. The only way to develop deep familiarity is to read the case several times. The following suggestions will help guide your reading:

- As you begin, take note of your first impression. What excites you? What bothers you? With whom did you relate? Subsequent readings may change your answers to these questions, so it's important to jot down your initial reactions to use as diagnostic tools. Initially they help you gauge your values and empathic response to the case. Later they may be key in helping you understand participants' starting points in the discussion.

- Since each case has many layers of meaning, each reading yields more information and understanding. As you read, ask yourself "What is this a case of?" and "What are the different ways to interpret this case?" Also note the descriptive words, key phrases, and dialogue used, especially early in the case, as the teacher–author introduces students or events.

- Reread the case with specific objectives in mind. Use one reading to identify teaching and learning issues and another to look for sociological impact—for example, how will events described in the case affect this student's capacity to contribute to the classroom community? A third reading can focus on the teacher's role—what professional issues are at stake? The more perspectives you have on the case, the better equipped you'll be to prompt broad-ranging discussion, thus reinforcing the idea that there is no one "right answer." Try to keep group participation balanced. Should one person's viewpoint tend to dominate, your suggestion of another lens to look through can draw out participants whose knowledge and experience make them identify with the case in an entirely different way.

- Look for pressure or stress points in the case—instances when a teacher is confronted by angry students, puzzled by a dilemma, or experiencing doubt or remorse about his actions. These events serve as teachable moments in the discussion. For example, in "Silences: The Case of the Invisible Boy," a crisis is followed by a catharsis for the teacher. If you prompt teachers to explore different interpretations of this event, they may come to understand why the crisis occurred. This insight can help them avert a similar situation in their classrooms.

- Look for subtle cues. Cases like "My Struggle With Sharon" overtly raise an interpersonal problem with a particular student. But a deeper understanding of student and teacher actions requires examining the narrative's details, perhaps making paragraph-by-paragraph notations. In many of the cases, information about individuals' perspectives is couched in subtle details. The group needs to look beneath the surface of what occurred. What might have happened if the teacher had perceived the student differently? What might the teacher have done, and how might the student have responded?

Using the teaching notes. This guide's teaching notes are resources designed to help you plan each case discussion. As analytic interpretations, they alert you in advance to potential problem areas. They examine key issues and sometimes add information not provided by the case's author.

Though the teaching notes are structured to help you analyze specific issues and provide examples of probing questions, they are *not* designed to give you a particular pathway for moving a group through the case. Instead, they are meant to help you make your own plan for discussion, from which you can deviate as you ascertain the group's direction with the discussion. Anticipating this, you can use the notes to identify stages of discussion and plan probing questions that enable participants to view the case through different lenses. Just as you customize case selection and sequence, you'll want to tailor questions to suit the profile of your particular group or school.

Planning the physical space. The arrangement of the physical space for discussions can either encourage intimate participation or discourage it. We have found that a U-shaped arrangement with participants seated at tables on the outside of the U works best. This arrangement enables participants to maintain eye contact with one another during a discussion and allows the facilitator to move within the circle at will. We ask participants to write their first names on the front of a folded index card and place it on the table in front of them. We also place either a board or easel with chart paper at the head of the U for recording major points made during the discussion. This enables participants to see how the discussion is progressing.

Providing adequate time. It takes time to peel away the surface layers of the cases and get to the underlying problems. If you allow two hours for case discussions, you should have adequate time to delve deeply into most of the cases. But what if you have only an hour to an hour and a half? This doesn't mean you shouldn't try to discuss any cases, but you *will* have to plan your time accordingly. One suggestion is to distribute the case before the actual discussion and ask participants to read it carefully, jotting down questions and noting issues *before* class.

The practice of coming to a session prepared to discuss a case is desirable even if you don't have a time crunch. In preservice education, teacher educators frequently ask students to prepare a preanalysis of a case before class and a postanalysis after the discussion. Pre- and postanalyses enable participants and teachers to track how the discussion influenced participants' insights into each case.

If you're pressed for time, it's important to keep one eye on the clock. It's easy to become caught up in one section of the discussion and run out of time before you complete all the parts you had planned. Stopping a discussion before you can bring it to closure is often more harmful than cutting short a particular section midway through the discussion.

DYNAMICS OF THE GROUP PROCESS

A successful discussion requires a climate of trust, acceptance of differing communication styles, and clearly defined roles and ground rules.

Establishing trust. Successful case discussion can take place only in a climate of trust. How can you help ensure that participants feel safe enough to risk exposing their opinions to others' judgment?

You'll need to consider many factors: physical setting, use of space, seating arrangement, your style of leading discussion, and group size. Perhaps most important, however, is the life experience of group members. Each participant brings to the group her personal values, attitudes, and beliefs—both conscious and unconscious. Trust will be affected by unspoken concerns, such as fears of being perceived by peers as an inadequate teacher who has problems in her classroom.

The clearer the structure and the more secure you are in the role of facilitator, the better the chances of developing a safe climate and productive discussion. Whenever possible, create groups that include individuals with differing life experiences, so participants can learn from each other.

In a group with well-established trust, the case discussion provides diverse participants a chance to reveal more of themselves and be better understood. In some instances a catharsis occurs and must be handled delicately. It is also important for the facilitator to be aware that established roles among members of a given group may create an obstacle to open discussion because of people's fixed opinions about each other.

Communication styles. Since people have different cultural values about communicating, it's important to note that participation may be unbalanced. Case discussion asks us to think about our reactions to characters in the case. The degree to which people are willing to reveal their values or beliefs is often a function of their style of communication.

Some participants will find it easy to talk openly and debate the topics; others won't. Some will be aggressive; others will hold back until they hear the rest of the group's opinions. Some will want to speak first; others will need prodding to speak at all. Some will disagree openly, others indirectly. These styles reflect not only personality, but culture. In classrooms we often subscribe to a particular model of communication—that you speak up when you disagree. However, to some cultures and individuals, it may be inappropriate to express disagreement.

As the facilitator, you must create a cross-cultural climate, which requires encouraging a variety of opinions through questioning and framing differing perspectives for examining the case. It also means watching people's body language so you won't lose the chance when a quiet person is about to say something. You can step in and gently silence interrupters. ("Susan hasn't had a chance to share her ideas about the story, so let's give her that time.")

Rules and roles. To establish a climate that is supportive of meaningful discussion, it's crucial that all participants understand the goals of the discussion, ground rules, and role of the facilitator.

Case discussion goals. A first step in leading a discussion is presenting the goals of the case seminar:

- To frame and reframe problems in each case

- To explore and analyze multiple viewpoints in each case

- To connect issues in the cases with participants' teaching situations and develop a repertoire of strategies to use in dealing with such issues

- To stimulate collaborative reflection and strategic introspection of one's own practice

- To develop collegiality and a shared understanding among participants

Ground rules for participants. Participants must overcome the notion that there is only one acceptable way to analyze each case. Instead, the aim is to foster an ethos of critical inquiry that encourages multiple interpretations, conflicting opinions, and equal participation. Clear ground rules can help set the stage for this kind of discourse:

- Respect each member's contribution and point of view and listen carefully.

- Do not interrupt! Wait for speakers to finish their statements before responding.

Role of the facilitator. To support these ground rules, facilitators should:

- Ensure equal and full participation by keeping track of those who want to speak and making sure each has a chance.

- Encourage quiet members to contribute and tactfully redirect those who dominate.

- At suitable points, synthesize key ideas; help clarify those that are misunderstood.

- Model candor, courtesy, and respect, and remind participants of ground rules whenever necessary.

- Avoid being the adviser each time someone makes a comment. At times be a blank screen, offering others the opportunity to respond.

LEADING THE DISCUSSION

Although you may have more expertise than the group you are working with, as *facilitator* you should not assume the role of expert during a case discussion. Rather, your responsibility is to elicit alternative perspectives and help participants analyze them. You should take the stance of an active listener, reflecting by your words and body language that you heard, understood, and accepted what the speaker communicated. You should also have at your disposal a set of probing questions that help expose, clarify, and challenge assumptions and proposed strategies that participants raise during the discussion (see teaching notes for examples of questions).

If members in your group appear to accept ideas before reflecting on different perspectives, you may offer other perspectives for their consideration. Your goal, however, is not to lead them to a specific point of view, but to help them come to their own conclusions about what is best for their students. One of the most difficult aspects of leading case discussions—especially for new discussion leaders—is the possibility that participants may leave a meeting with what appears to you to be the wrong point of view. You may feel compelled to give the "correct" answers, as if there is one best solution. Instead, try not to show impatience with teachers' views. Changing beliefs takes time, and being told what to believe is rarely effective. Individuals come with their own set of experiences that help shape their beliefs. They need time to evaluate these during case discussions and later in their classrooms. The cases in this volume are constructed and sequenced so that participants and facilitators have numerous opportunities to revisit the same issues (see Table 1 in the Introduction).

THE OPENING

When beginning a new group, remember that group members may need to get acquainted. Field testing showed that allowing time for participants to introduce themselves, or even using a simple icebreaker, sets a comfortable and warm climate and pays off later. If a group is going to meet several times, it is worthwhile to allow substantial time during the first session for getting acquainted, going over rules and roles, and discussing the purpose of using cases in teacher education.

How do you begin a discussion? Your opening questions are important; they set the tone and scope of the entire discussion. Experimenting with ways to make your openings as flexible and participatory as possible should be one of your goals.

One opening approach is to establish facts by asking one or two people to summarize what actually happened in the case, then asking others to join in. Asking for the facts of the case is a comfortable way to enter the discussion because it enables everyone to begin the discussion with a shared sense of what happened and emphasizes the importance of differentiating fact from interpretation. Sometimes, however, participants become frustrated with this exercise and want to jump right in and get to the provocative issues. If this happens, you will have to judge how important it is to establish facts before delving into larger issues. You can always return to the facts by asking factual questions throughout the discussion and referring back to the text periodically to gather evidence.

Another way to open a discussion is to ask participants to work in pairs for five minutes to generate key issues and questions raised by the case and record their results on a board or easel chart paper before fleshing out any issues. (If you want to begin with facts, you can use this approach after the facts have been established.) There are many advantages to this approach: (1) participants can refer to the list during the discussion, making sure that all points were addressed; (2) you and the group acquire a sense of the range of interpretations before discussion begins; and (3) you convey the idea that there are many ways to look at the case, thus ensuring that the discussion doesn't become fixated on a single view. This approach works especially well when you meet with a new or particularly large group because all members become engaged immediately in discussing the issues. The pair work also serves to break the ice for those who are hesitant to talk in large groups and makes them more inclined to speak up in the larger setting than they might otherwise be.

After completing the list of issues and questions, ask the group to decide where *they* wish to start the discussion. This sends a subtle message that you respect the group's agenda and won't impose your own. Some teachers reported that this gesture was important; it appears to empower some to speak up who might otherwise remain silent.

A third approach to beginning the discussion is to provide a focus question and immediately examine a key issue. If you choose this tactic, be sure to consider your opening question carefully, because it is likely to set the tone for the entire discussion. The advantage of starting with a focus question is that the discussion usually gets off to a lively beginning. The tradeoff is that it may prevent some participants from bringing up their own issues. It may also convey the perception that you have a fixed agenda for the discussion.

CORE OF THE DISCUSSION

Once the initial focus of the discussion is established, we suggest the following discussion components:

- **Analysis**. Analyze the problem(s) from the viewpoints of the different actors in the case, using the notes as a guide to the analysis. Adequate analysis often takes *at least* half the discussion.

- **Evaluation**. Examine the teacher's strategies for handling the problem(s).

- **Alternative Solutions**. Generate alternative strategies for handling the problems, making sure to consider the risks, benefits, and long-term consequences of each.

- **Principles of Practice**. Formulate some generalizations about good practice based on this case discussion, prior discussions, teachers' experience, and their prior theoretical understanding.

- **"What Is This a Case Of**?" Moving up the ladder of abstraction, link this case to more general categories; rich cases are, by nature, "of" many things.

Though this pathway appears to be linear, in reality, discussions rarely follow such a straight path. One aspect of the discussion, however, should follow sequentially. We emphasize the necessity of adequately analyzing the issues in the cases—from a variety of perspectives—*before* evaluating how the teacher handled the problems and generating alternative strategies. In our experience, educators sometimes make quick judgments and begin generating alternative solutions before adequately analyzing the problems.

In a typical discussion, the initial focus is on the particularities of the case and an analysis of what happened. In the diagnosis of what went wrong, participants' comments often reflect personal experience (particularly if they are experienced teachers) and theoretical understanding: "The teacher didn't adequately take advantage of Dennis's contribution to the group as a status intervention"; "The teacher didn't prepare her class adequately for their group task"; "The teacher didn't tailor her assessment to what students learned in their group." Experienced teachers or novices with some classroom experience often enrich the discussion with stories of their own experience.

The effectiveness of the analysis depends to a great extent on your repertoire of questioning techniques that encourage reflection. Different types of questions (e.g., open-ended, diagnostic, challenging, prediction, and hypothetical) serve different purposes. The teaching notes in this volume contain numerous examples of types of questions. As facilitator, you should be prepared to follow participants' responses with probing questions that deepen their reflection (see Figure 1 for a typology of probing questions). When participants begin to ask questions of one another, rather than continually orienting their remarks toward you, this is a sign of growth among the group.

Figure 1

Typology of Questions

Adapted from: Christensen, C. R., et al. (1991). *Education for judgment: The artistry of discussion leadership.* Boston: Harvard University Press.

Open-ended questions: What are your reactions to the case about the teacher who cried in front of her students? What aspects of the problem were of greatest interest to you?

Diagnostic questions: What is your analysis of the problem? What conclusions can you draw from the data?

Information-seeking questions: What is the range of reading test scores in your class this year?

Challenge (testing) questions: Why do you believe that? What evidence supports your conclusion? What arguments can be developed to counter that point of view?

Action questions: What needs to be done to implement the plans in the teacher's planning book?

Questions on priority and sequence: Given the failure of Mr. Hanson's smartest students, what is the first step to be taken? The second? And the third?

Prediction questions: If your conclusions are correct, what might be the reactions of your students?

Hypothetical questions: What would have happened if Ms. Masterson had not asked her mentor for help? Would Bart have succeeded if he had not been appointed as leader in his group?

Questions of extension: What are the implications of your conclusions about why this group remained uncooperative?

Questions of generalization: Based on the discussion and your past experience, what principles of teaching and learning should you consider when deciding whether to intervene in a group's discussion.

Figure 1. Typology of Questions

Ethos of inquiry. One of the most important tasks of the facilitator is to create an ethos of inquiry—a group spirit that is not limited merely to exchanging opinions, but rather leads to substantive learning. Accomplishing this task requires remembering that the focal point of a case discussion—the personalized narrative—can be both a hook and a pitfall. The detailed individual story draws people in and prompts them to share their own stories, especially since they often just left their classrooms. But this level of discussion can be so absorbing that the group fails to realize that the point is to generate principles, or sets of practices, or new ways of thinking that can be tested across cases and in the classroom.

The facilitator's challenge is, first, to build an ample world of ideas for the group to explore, then to move discussion up and down a ladder of exploration: up to higher principles, back down to very discrete practices, then up again—in other words, to repeatedly move from the level of opinion swap to the desired level of applied knowledge. How do you do that? How do you get people to deduce principles from experiences they're discussing, to move away, come back, then generalize again?

- Try not to become emotionally involved in what's being said. You will be more effective if you keep some distance and continually analyze how the discussion is going. Pay particular attention to equitable participation.

- Periodically tie up loose ends, summarize what's been learned, and move along to the next increment. This keeps group members from repeatedly coming back to the same point or digressing so far that their talk no longer relates to the case.

- After evaluating how a teacher in the case dealt with a particular problem, ask what alternative strategies the teacher could have used and analyze the risks and benefits of each. Such questions can inspire teachers to make judicious changes in their own situations.

- At opportune moments, ask participants to come up with generalizations or principles based on this and other case discussions and their experience. This develops their capacity to transfer what they learn from the analysis of a particular case to similar situations they are likely to meet in their classrooms.

- Bear in mind that you are teaching the skills of case analysis. Ultimately, you are moving participants toward applying what they're learning to their teaching behaviors, but only in-depth analysis allows that learning to occur, and the skills required take time to develop.

The possibility of establishing a true ethos of inquiry is enhanced if you structure the case-based curriculum. As explained above, this involves assigning other readings that play off the issues and questions embedded in each case. When discussion takes place in such a structure, the group will not be confined to talking only about what they think happened in the narrative or their personal values or beliefs, but can explore other people's ways of looking at a given topic.

Your larger goal is to extend this approach beyond the single case discussion to the entire course or curriculum. Over time, discussion will have covered a family of cases, which then can be crisscrossed, or compared with each other. At the end, you should be able to engage participants in framing guiding principles that they now feel would apply, not just to teaching students like those in the cases, but to teaching in any setting where issues about groupwork come into play.

The greatest challenge of the case approach is that each discussion is different and takes on a life of its own. At times the discussion may appear at an impasse, or participants may be ignoring information you feel is key to understanding the case's problems or dilemmas. At such times you need to shift the topic. One way is to say you've spent a lot of time discussing a particular topic, then ask about viewing it from another perspective (give an example). Another tack is to play devil's advocate, then introduce the missing issue as a counterpoint. Or you might elicit questions about a quote from the case. Occasionally it may be useful to push ahead a discussion by giving a two- or three-minute mini-lecture based on the teaching notes or other scholarly sources. (This can be risky if it is perceived as too directive; it may also limit discussion.) Another strategy is to incorporate activities such as role playing and/or discussion in structured small groups, which can offer a welcome change of pace.

Be sensitive to the possibility that there may be tension between your agenda for a case discussion and the group's. This requires a delicate balance. If you merely follow where the participants want to take the discussion, you abrogate your role as a teacher; but if you stick to your discussion plan without letting participants move in a direction they prefer, you communicate that you are in control and they might hesitate to bring up their issues and concerns. One way to get around this dilemma is to look for opportunities to build on participants' ideas, rather than raising new ideas yourself. Also, remind them that in your role as facilitator, you will challenge their ideas and push them to defend their views, regardless of their position. Ultimately we are trying to move participants from reflection to problem solving and a willingness to investigate their own classroom practice.

CLOSING THE CASE DISCUSSION

Another major challenge is helping participants synthesize and reflect on what they learned from the entire discussion. Participants should have the opportunity to identify new understandings as well as unresolved conflicts and questions before the discussion is over.

One approach is asking participants to reflect on the case and respond to the question "What is this a case of?" This question, which began as a suggestion from Lee Shulman, is the theme that weaves through all our casework. It asks teachers to characterize a particular case in relation to other cases, to their own experience, and to the conceptual or abstract categories with which they are familiar. Shulman suggests that it is a way of encouraging participants to move between the memorable particularities of cases and the powerful simplifications of principles and theory (L. Shulman, 1996).

. . . the key move made in teaching with cases occurs when instructor and students explore the question "What is this a case of?" As they wrestle with this question, they move the case in two directions simultaneously. They connect this narrative to their remembered (personal) experiences or to vicariously experienced cases written or recounted by others, thus relating this particular case to other specific cases. They also connect this narrative to categories of experience, to theoretical classifications through which they organize and make sense of their world. (pp. 208–209)

In our experience, closing a discussion with "What is this a case of?" has been extremely valuable in helping participants move away from the particularities of a specific case and begin to identify the variety of categories that the case represents. Please note that rich cases are usually "of" many things. Often what they are "of" depends upon the nature of a particular discussion and the experience of its participants.

Other ways of bringing the discussion to closure include asking the students to spend a few minutes doing a "freewrite," responding to such questions as: What did you learn from this case discussion? Do you have lingering questions? What part of the discussion did you find most challenging? How can you relate what we discussed to your own experience? Some people appreciate the opportunity to synthesize their thoughts in writing before sharing them with the larger group.

Another approach is to divide the group into pairs to share what they learned, relate it to their own experience, and brainstorm what they would do differently. After the pairs meet, bring the group back together and ask one member of each pair to report key ideas they discussed.

A final tactic is simply to ask what principles and/or generalizations participants can generate from this and other discussions and what questions remain unanswered. Record this information; you may want to compare it with a previous list of principles.

DISCUSSION STAGES AND STRUGGLES

No group achieves a climate of trust without a series of struggles. Facilitators need to be aware that groups undergo developmental growth. Along the way, people shift roles and become more at ease with differences of opinion. Part of your job is to create a nonjudgmental climate that supports this progression.

The group's comfort level is directly related to your own. As your skills develop, your confidence grows and your anxieties diminish. Your equanimity then sets a tone supportive of people whose opinions may differ strongly from yours. Providing informal opportunities for socializing also helps establish warmth that carries over into the discussions.

Once established, a climate of trust may lead a group member to make a personal revelation in the course of explaining his reaction to a case. Such moments can be fragile; your support and the respect of the group are crucial. Such moments can also be breakthroughs, moving the group to a deeper level of discussion and creating strong group bonds.

We noted earlier that people participate in different ways, which may be related to racial and ethnic perceptions and roles. As the facilitator, you play a strong part in determining who dominates the discussion and who

is not contributing. Take time to examine that role. This requires a sort of self-diagnosis, using questions analogous to those used in searching for meaning in a case. Immediately after reading each case, ask yourself, "What did I feel about the story? What did I really like or not like?" Then step back and ask, "To whom do I find myself asking questions? Do I have favorites?"

Be aware of how your style of communicating influences your responses to participants' behaviors: who do you feel is getting carried away and who do you feel comfortable with? Your responses allow or impede productive discourse. In short, your best diagnostic tool for knowing whether the group is progressing toward nonjudgmental discourse is your own comfort level.

The case discussions in *Groupwork in Diverse Classrooms* offer teachers insights into effectively utilizing small groups. But that potential can be realized only through each group's process of reflection. If successful, the group may become a microcosm of what we're trying to accomplish in our classrooms: to reach a place where inquiry, reflection, respect, and equal participation are the norm.

PART II: TEACHING NOTES

Case 1

When Do You Intervene?

This case typifies classic dilemmas that go to the heart of groupwork: while students are working in their groups, when is it appropriate for teachers to intervene? How should they intervene? These are complex questions and appear in several cases in this volume. On one hand, when teachers delegate authority to students for their own learning in small groups, students are empowered to be actively involved in their own learning and can benefit from collegial interaction with their peers. On the other hand, teachers feel they are ultimately responsible for their students' learning. What happens when kids may misunderstand basic concepts and teach their misconceptions to others?

In this situation, students had previously divided into groups to research the island of Borneo and become experts on particular topics. As we enter the narrative, the teacher reconfigures the students into jigsaw groups so that each newly formed group has one expert from each topic. During jigsaw, the "experts" share their knowledge with the others so that all can develop a deep understanding of the material. However, when two of the experts appear to present inaccurate information to their respective groups, the teacher struggles to figure out how to intervene. She seeks to prevent misunderstandings without harming either the self-esteem of individual experts or the spirit of community that had been developed within the class.

CONTEXT

This fifth/sixth grade combination classroom set in an inner-city school participated in the Fostering a Community of Learners (FCL) research project created by Ann Brown and Joe Campione at the University of California, Berkeley. FCL is an approach to groupwork in which deep disciplinary understanding and the development of skills of critical literacy are central.

Students engage in collaborative research, share their information and understandings through jigsaw and other activities, and apply what they have learned to a new and more difficult task that is reported in a public exhibition or performance. In an FCL classroom, groupwork activities elegantly synthesize several highly regarded approaches to groupwork, e.g., jigsaw (Aronson), reciprocal teaching (Palincsar and Brown), group investigation (Sharan), and writing process groups (National Writing Project).

QUESTIONS AND ISSUES

This case raises fundamental issues and beliefs about teaching and learning. Reactions to the basic dilemma varied widely. Whereas some teachers identified strongly with this teacher's questions, others wondered why she even wrote the case: "What's the problem? If you see that someone is giving the wrong information, of course you must correct the mistakes." Thus the case is about much more than groupwork: it is about how students gain knowledge and how teachers foster that process. The case facilitator may want to consider the background of the group members and their familiarity with *constructivist* models of learning, in which the active development of meaning by the learner is seen as essential for deep understanding (as opposed to *transmission* models of learning, in which teachers tell and students remember). The decision to use this case, the intended purposes, and the kinds of questions to have in mind as a facilitator will be influenced by the background of the group. Is the group likely to challenge the teacher's approach, or is it ready to consider subtle details of how the teacher facilitates learning? Do group members agree with this teacher's belief that "people don't hear something until they are ready"?

Purpose of groupwork

What do you think is the purpose of groupwork in this classroom? How does it impact student learning and the development of classroom community? What kind of community is the teacher trying to create with her students? How does this teacher's conception of groupwork compare to your own?

Multiple roles of teachers during groupwork

The role of the teacher in this classroom differs dramatically from the traditional role in which a teacher's primary responsibility is to transmit information. How does this teacher see her role? How does she illustrate this in the narrative? How does her role definition inherently create tensions during groupwork? What is your definition of the role of a teacher? How similar or different is it from this teacher's conception?

Intervention or not?

As the teacher articulately describes, "When students emerge as 'experts' in a domain, sometimes their newly formed theories are erroneous." Examine the two problematic jigsaw situations, first individually and then comparatively. What actually happened in each situation? What were the perceived errors that each expert made? How important were the errors to students' understanding of DDT and its use? Was the teacher–author accurate in her perception? Several biology teachers in our pilot test felt that Doranne might have understood DDT more than the teacher gave her credit for. How might the teacher have discovered this?

What did the teacher do in each situation? It might be useful to refer to the text for the teacher's exact words. Were there any apparent differences in her approach to each intervention? If so, how might students have interpreted her questions differently? What might have happened if the teacher had ignored these errors? What alternate strategies could she have taken? What are the risks and benefits of each strategy? This is a rich opportunity to explore considerations and approaches in handling perceived misconceptions and the trade-offs associated with each.

The teacher discovered Doranne's apparent misunderstanding when she responded inaccurately to a question about her paper. Some participants may point out that the teacher could have intervened by correcting the paper. Why was the paper allowed to reach the jigsaw with inaccurate information? This could open the door for an interesting discussion. What is a teacher's responsibility for the accuracy of a group's paper? Are there situations in which it is appropriate to allow misunderstandings in a paper? Why?

Issues of power and status

This teacher was concerned about power and status issues in her classroom. Teachers can find opportunities to raise a student's status by publicly recognizing that student's contribution. They can also lower a student's status inadvertently with inappropriate interventions.

In this case, the teacher thought Doranne had a "potentially serious misunderstanding" about DDT after hearing her presentation during a jigsaw. At this point, the teacher had to make a split-second decision. Should she wait until the jigsaw was over and deal with the misunderstanding during a whole-class lesson, or should she intervene on the spot? These are the kinds of quick decisions teachers have to make hundreds of times during a day. This time she decided to question Doranne immediately because she felt Doranne "was very self-confident." Yet after the teacher's intervention, Doranne didn't speak again during the jigsaw session. This raises some interesting questions. Does this experience imply that one shouldn't tell a student she is wrong? How and under what circumstances do you tell a student she is wrong? Psychologists caution teachers against expecting more from some students than others. Lower expectations can become a self-fulfilling prophecy, lowering opportunities for some kids to learn. How does this theory inform our understanding of the teacher's dilemma? How do issues of power affect the learning community of this and other classrooms?

Principles of teaching and learning

How typical are these problems for you in your classroom? When presented with a situation in which it appears that small groups of students are either missing the point or discussing inaccurate information, what should you do? How do you weigh the chance of developing misconceptions with the chance of damaging a student's self-esteem? What principles of teaching and learning should you consider when deciding whether to intervene in a group's discussion?

Case 2

Groupwork? Rats!

This veteran elementary school science teacher struggles to expand her students' conception of learning. In her quest for developing a constructivist classroom where students take responsibility for their own learning, she creates rotating learning stations that incorporate both text-oriented activities and hands-on science investigations. But she is surprised to discover that the students thought they learned more from whole-class instruction and traditional reading and question-answer activities than from hands-on science activities. During the narrative, she questions her classroom organization, methods, and procedures and paves the way for rich analysis and discussion about these issues. (Many of the questions raised in this case are similar to those described by the high school chemistry teacher in Case 4.)

CONTEXT

After 16 years as a primary teacher in an inner-city elementary school, this teacher has a new role this year as science specialty teacher for 350 students in grades 1 through 5. She feels constrained by 50-minute periods and wonders how she will "ever learn their names, much less facilitate learning the scientific method in a science lab."

QUESTIONS AND ISSUES

This teacher has thought a lot about the kinds of instructional activities that lead to real learning. What does she mean by *real learning*? What do you think it is? The teacher appears to favor group investigations over whole-group activities and provides her rationale in the last paragraph of her case. Do you agree with her analysis? What do you think are the advantages and limitations of each form of instruction? How might both kinds of instruction interact to support each other?

Examining the task

This teacher used groupwork for two kinds of tasks. Let's examine each one individually.

The mapping task. What was the teacher's purpose for the mapping task? What did she hope would happen? What actually happened? How did the students respond? Many science teachers take special precautions to teach their students how to work in a science lab and with animals. How did this teacher prepare the students for their observational task? What were the consequences for inappropriate behavior?

The teacher wondered whether her emphasis on working together during this task affected the group negatively. What do you think? How might you have handled a similar situation? She noted that earlier log entries by students revealed that the group had been "cooperative and engaged in their observation." In looking at the entries, do you agree with her assessment? Why?

The teacher noted that she hadn't rushed over when the group began to experience problems because she wanted to "promote and honor the students' ability to find their own way to work together." What are the trade-offs for teacher intervention in this case? What would you have done? What are the risks and benefits of your proposed strategy?

Text-related task. The teacher said the text-related task was similar to the kind of work students routinely did in their classrooms—looking up answers to questions in a book. She thought the task was dull compared to the hands-on activities at the other tables and was surprised that the students appeared to like it. Yet in analyzing the task, we quickly see that this was no simple question-answer task that came from a textbook. Rather, it was a creative assignment that demanded cooperation and collaboration among students. Examine the task. Note particularly: student-generated questions, use of multiple resources, evidence of distributed expertise (pairs of students working from different resources), and evidence of interdependence through consensus and helping behaviors. What did the teacher hope to accomplish from this task? What actually happened?

How did individual students, especially John, respond? How did they and the teacher assess their work? What do you think of the design of this task? Would you call it a group investigation?

Comparing the tasks. How would you compare the mapping and text-related tasks? What kind of preparation is needed for each? How is each task related to real learning?

Assessment

One of the most important and difficult challenges in groupwork is developing appropriate assessment procedures for individuals and groups. What methods did the teacher use to assess the mapping and text-related tasks? What other kinds of assessments could she have used? How would/do you assess group tasks in your classroom?

Classroom organization

This science lab/classroom is rather atypical in an elementary setting, yet it raises some interesting questions about classroom organization. The class is organized in learning centers, where students get a chance to revisit a concept through several group activities. On occasion, the teacher breaks up the routine and provides whole-class instruction, but it appears she does not like it. What are the advantages and limitations of this kind of arrangement from the teacher's perspective? From the students' perspective? From your perspective? Is it possible to have kids work through creative learning stations and end up learning nothing? What has to happen for real learning to occur? How would/do you organize your class to achieve real learning?

How can you expand childrens' perceptions of real learning?

The teacher describes her frustration with her students' limited ideas of what "real learning" is. In a personal communication with one of the case editors, she noted, "If kids have one perception of learning, it creates real boundaries around what they consider learning." How does that perception interfere with more hands-on modes of learning? How can you expand their perception of what real learning is? What principles of teaching and learning would you draw on to answer these questions?

Case 3

Poor Period 3!

The eighth grade social studies teacher in this case explores whether groupwork is ever an inappropriate teaching strategy. She describes a class that is difficult to manage because it has a "disproportionate number of emotionally needy individuals." After a particularly unproductive groupwork lesson, the teacher attempts several strategies to improve the situation; the strategies are met with varying degrees of success. This case offers many opportunities to discuss the purposes of groupwork, establishment of a classroom climate for productive groupwork, and strategies for classroom management of groups.

CONTEXT

This 20-year elementary and middle school veteran teaches eighth grade social studies at a middle school in a middle income suburban neighborhood. The student population is diverse—50% Latino, 40% Caucasian, and the remaining 10% a mix of African American, Asian American, and Filipino. The teacher describes the students as coming from "low–middle class neighborhoods." At this school, the students and teachers at each grade level are divided into two teams. A team of teachers teaches all the subjects to the same group of approximately 170 students. This teacher team comprises six teachers—two in language arts, one in math, one in science, one in social studies, and one computer/special support teacher. The author of this case is the social studies teacher for all 170 students on the team. In any given class, there are a number of students designated as "sheltered" because they are in the process of learning English and require additional language instruction support. In addition, all special education students in the eighth grade are mainstreamed into this team. There are nine special education students as well as a full-time teaching aide in the class described.

QUESTIONS AND ISSUES

The title, prologue, and background section of this case vividly portray this teacher's third period. How does this teacher describe the class? (Probe for specific details, e.g., "poor," "my match," "disturbing chemistry," "torment each other.") What kind of mood or classroom atmosphere does she depict in the opening dialogue? How do you think she feels when she is teaching the class? How do you think students feel during class? She describes this class as "her match." What are the implications of the adversarial metaphor she employs to describe this class?

What does she believe is the cause of the problems in the class? (Probe for "disproportionate number of emotionally needy individuals.") What is your analysis of the problem this class presents?

Have you ever had a class like hers? How did you cope?

Purposes for groupwork

Groupwork can serve many different pedagogical purposes—for example, enhancing deep content knowledge and promoting higher-order thinking, language learning, and pro-social behavior. What are this teacher's purposes for groupwork? Of these, which seems most important to her? As you examine the case as a whole, in your estimation, which of these does she fulfill?

The groupwork task

The teacher weaves into her narrative a description of a sample lesson, a role-play activity called Elementary Eagle. What does she expect students to learn through this activity? In your opinion, is this a sound groupwork task? Justify your opinion.

Roles in groupwork

In this case, the teacher has assigned each student a specific procedural role. For instance, she mentions designating a harmonizer and a facilitator; other roles commonly assigned are reporter, recorder, and materials manager. These procedural roles are assigned so that the students collectively assume responsibility for keeping the group on task and working productively. They are designed to free the teacher from the burden of management (e.g., seeing that each group knows what to do or that it has the proper materials) and thereby afford her opportunities to attend to students' thinking and learning.

How do students appear to handle the responsibilities of their procedural roles? How well prepared do the students appear to be to perform their roles? What are some ways you can introduce students to roles? How does your use of roles compare with this teacher's?

Just as crafting groups can present a thicket of decisions, so too can the assignment of roles to students. How do you think this teacher decided which students should play which roles? How do you think the students felt about the roles they were assigned?

When describing the task, the teacher mentions roles each student must assume in order to complete the task (e.g., fisherman, farmer, carpenter, merchant, or soldier). How do these roles contrast with the procedural roles (e.g., facilitator, harmonizer, etc.)?

Classroom management

Introducing groupwork can sometimes exacerbate classroom management difficulties. Several episodes in the narrative suggest that the teacher has some difficulty managing this class. What specific inappropriate student behaviors does the teacher mention? How does she handle these students and situations? To what extent is groupwork a factor in the disruptive episodes? How would you handle these students and situations? What advice regarding appropriate response could you offer this teacher?

Debriefing discussion

A debriefing discussion often follows a groupwork lesson, with topics ranging from summary and analysis of content learned to groupwork process. What aspects of groupwork does this teacher address in her debriefing? How do you think students responded to the debriefing discussion? In your opinion, what impact will this discussion have on future groupwork lessons? How would you have conducted this discussion?

Strategies to improve groupwork

After struggling through the Elementary Eagle lesson, the teacher attempts several strategies to improve groupwork in this class. What are the strategies? How does she assess their relative impact on the class? Can you suggest other strategies that might have worked with this class? What are the trade-offs associated with her various strategies? With those you may have suggested?

A cooperative atmosphere

How does the teacher explain why her period 3 students cannot create a "cooperative atmosphere"? (Probe for examples—"emotionally needy," "lack experience in small group interaction," "lack self-esteem.") Based on the information, how do you explain the class's uncooperative atmosphere? In your opinion, what can be done to improve the tenor of period 3?

In the epilogue, the teacher observes that creating an atmosphere of trust is both time consuming and necessary for productive groupwork. How do you assess her conclusion? Aside from trust, are there other attributes you feel characterize a cooperative classroom? What advice can you offer others about how to establish a cooperative classroom? What trade-offs does a teacher make by taking the time to build a cooperative atmosphere?

Professional development

At several points in the narrative, the teacher refers to her professional development experiences with groupwork. How does she describe those experiences? How does she draw upon what she learned in profes-

sional development seminars? (Probe for examples—
"conversion to groupwork," "persist as I was trained,"
"clinical answers.") Given her statements about professional development and descriptions of her teaching,
what do you think are her assumptions about her role
and the students' role during groupwork?

Case 4

Do You Let Kids Fail?

After teaching chemistry in a traditional manner for seven years, this teacher tries a new approach focused on independent learning, problem solving, and groupwork. Whereas some groups blossom on their own, others struggle. One group in particular appears to resent the teacher's unwillingness to provide direction for the group task and fails to develop its final presentation. The teacher is left wondering whether it was right of her to let the group fail. This case and Case 10 question how teachers can motivate students to assume responsibility for their learning.

CONTEXT

This teacher teaches in a suburban school that has some of the richest and poorest students in the Bay Area. Her chemistry classes reflect the school's diverse student body. Recently, the teacher added Complex Instruction to her teaching repertoire.

QUESTIONS AND ISSUES

The teacher–author is surprised and disappointed by the extent to which the students depend on her to give or confirm the "right answer." Several teachers in our pilot project questioned this response. In most classrooms, teachers are designated authorities and teach the "right answer," and students have been led to expect that this kind of teaching represents good education. Unless we provide another model and convincing activities to support it, why should students think otherwise? If you want to radically change your teaching methods to a more constructivist approach that uses lots of groupwork, how can you motivate students to buy into that approach?

What is the teacher's philosophy of good teaching? Examine her background as depicted in the case. How did her own high school experience differ from the way she traditionally taught? How does it compare to your philosophy?

Purpose of groupwork

What do you think the teacher hoped to achieve through groupwork? Examine the first unit. How is it different from a more traditional unit? Were her aspirations realized in the unit? What evidence do you have to support your conjecture?

Student perceptions of the task

How did the students—particularly those in the problematic group—respond to the teacher's first unit? Why do you think Sarah and Roger responded as they did? It appears that the two other group members understood the main points of their section. They were the same students who were reluctant to go to the front of the class for their group's final presentation. How do you think they felt in this group? How could you provide support for these students?

Look at the text to examine how the teacher responded to their questions and biting comments such as, "You can't expect us to understand this stuff. That's why they hired *you* to be the teacher." These are difficult moments for any teacher. Evaluate the teacher's tactics. What alternate strategies could she have used? What are the risks and benefits to each one? It's more difficult to come up with real words than to propose a general strategy. What exactly would you say?

Teacher and student roles

Successful groupwork requires that students assume some responsibility for their learning. This teacher created new roles for herself and for her students.

Teacher role. This teacher defined her role as a facilitator or coach. As facilitator, she recommended resources and listened to the group's plan of action. When a group asked her to validate their action plan, she responded with questions for them to reflect on. Her refrain was, "Answer a question with a question." What are the benefits of this stance? Can you think of any problems with it? As you define your role, how does it compare with the way this teacher defined hers? Give some examples.

Student roles. To ensure that group members participated, the teacher assigned each member a specific role. These roles—facilitator and presentation specialist, reporter and homework specialist, encourager and evaluation specialist, and materials and equipment specialist—were designed to free the teacher from the burden of management. If students take responsibility for directions and materials, for example, it makes it possible for teachers to attend to students' thinking and learning. What are the advantages of these role assignments? Are there any disadvantages? What might happen if there were no role assignments?

Preparing students for groupwork

The narrative doesn't include a description of how the teacher introduced her approach to teaching, yet this doesn't mean she had no introduction. Since we can infer from the narrative that the new teaching methods were radically different from what the students were typically exposed to, it would have been important to motivate and prepare them for the new experience. How would you introduce this kind of teaching to students? What kinds of activities would you use to prepare them for cooperative and collaborative behavior in their groups (see Case 10)?

Assessment

Assessment is a theme in many of the cases in this volume. Teachers—especially secondary-school teachers—take accountability seriously and wonder how to assess group projects adequately. Examine the group evaluation sheet the teacher developed collaboratively with the class. What do you think of this as a group evaluation tool? No mention is made of any form of individual assessment for the unit. Do you think individual assessment is needed? If so, what form would it take?

Crafting groups

The issue of how to formulate a group runs through many of these cases (see, for example, Cases 7 and 10). This teacher took the time to craft groups in specific ways. What were her criteria? She wonders why this particular group of four was not working. What's your analysis of the problem? How would/do you group students in your classroom?

Action plan

Examine how the teacher handled the group's failure to complete its task. If you were the teacher, what would you have done? How would you have responded to the challenge "I guess Mrs. Stevens will have to teach this if anybody is going to learn anything about the effect of pressure"? Have students ever challenged you like this in your classroom? What did you do? As you think about the possibility of similar situations arising in your classroom, can you generalize about how to deal with these challenges?

Reflections

At the end of the case, the teacher raises two questions: (1) Why are the students who appear to have difficulty working in groups more motivated and involved when the class is taught in a traditional lecture/discussion mode? (2) How can I motivate students to take responsibility for their own learning? (These are similar to the questions raised in Case 2.) How would you respond to both questions?

Case 5

Exploring Alternative Assessment

In this case, a veteran science teacher delves into the serious dilemma of how to assess student learning that is the result of groupwork. As she talks about her dilemma, the author experiences a gamut of emotions: from acute anguish at the mere thought of evaluation, to exhilaration because her students were *doing* science, and deep astonishment that in spite of successful groupwork, students didn't perform any better than they had when they were using more traditional approaches.

After rethinking the connection between instruction and assessment and listening to her students' comments, the teacher decides to develop a new test that is closely linked to the instruction and to involve the students in the process. When the new test is administered, scores improve and the students feel that the new test assesses their learning better than the traditional one. For the teacher, the experience raises fundamental questions about assessment, traditional and alternative, and leads her to reexamine her philosophy about the goals and practices of student assessment.

CONTEXT

This case is from a suburban high school that has students from some of the richest and poorest neighborhoods in the area. The chemistry classes reflect the school's diverse student body. Recently, the teacher added Complex Instruction to her teaching repertoire. During the first month of school, she used this particular model of groupwork to teach a unit on density, which is typically a difficult concept for students to understand.

QUESTIONS AND ISSUES

Although the central dilemma raised by the author of this case is alternative assessment, because of the close connection among assessment, instruction, and instructional tasks, you may also wish to explore the learning tasks presented in the case.

Purposes of groupwork and examination of the task

After seven years of teaching, this teacher added Complex Instruction to her repertoire of teaching techniques. She created a four-day unit, using the curriculum design principles of this model of groupwork. In Complex Instruction, activities of a unit are organized around a central concept, question, or "big idea." As students rotate to complete the activities of a unit (hence the four days dedicated to it) they encounter this idea, question, or concept in different contexts or settings. Thus they have multiple opportunities to grapple with the material, to explore related questions, to look at different representations, and to think of different applications. In this case the teacher did not orient the students to the central concept before they began the activities. Rather, she planned for them to work with the concept of density as they performed the activities.

How and why would groupwork contribute to students' understanding of a difficult concept such as density? In what ways would the rotations contribute to deepening this understanding?

As mentioned, the teacher chose not to introduce the concept of density explicitly, probably to avoid preteaching the concept, thereby short-circuiting students' own discovery of the scientific properties of density. What are the advantages and disadvantages of this strategy? If you were teaching this unit, when would you choose to introduce a big idea or central concept? When would you leave it up to the students to gradually formulate their own theories and understanding?

Science teachers discussing this case were particularly intrigued by the following issues: What were the scientific objectives of the different tasks of the unit? How was the central concept of density reflected in each of these tasks? What would be the teacher's role in making the connection between these tasks and the central concept? Among the various tasks? Among density and other scientific phenomena or concepts?

How could the teacher use students' reports during the "scientific conventions" to make connections among the various activities, reinforce the central concept, and deepen students' understanding? How did students build upon their own work in the groups and their classmates' reports during the "scientific conventions"? (Probe for modified questions that were generated by the class.)

The teacher is pleasantly surprised by the metamorphosis her students underwent. (Probe for the participants to question whether these were the same students.) How do you account for this metamorphosis? Have participants look closely at the individual reports included in the case showing what students were required to discuss and consider.

What could the teacher mean when she said, "[Some] students refused to use the term 'mass' just a few days ago"? In your opinion, why was the difference between Coke and Diet Coke such an engaging question for them?

Depth versus breadth

Although pleased with how the unit went, the teacher is concerned about spending four days on one topic. Traditionally, she had spent only one period on the concept of density, because she was worried about the amount of material that needed to be covered in this chemistry class. Many teachers (especially at the secondary level) are deeply concerned with the tension between curriculum coverage and in-depth exploration of selected topics; in many cases teachers find they can't make a personal choice because of administrative edicts, pressures to prepare students for various kinds of tests, or department-level or grade-level decisions.

What are your thoughts about the dilemma of depth versus breadth? Under what circumstances, if any, do you have the freedom to make a choice between covering more material or exploring a concept in greater depth? How do pressures external to the classroom and to learning influence a teacher's decision? If you were to choose to spend a whole week on one topic (rather than one period as other teachers in your department or at your grade level do), how would you defend your decision to your colleagues? To your students? To their parents? What arguments would you bring before them?

The first quiz

Examine the quizzes at the end of the case. Why was the teacher astonished as she graded the quizzes? What made her think that her students would do any better this year than students had in previous years? As you think about the activities, the individual reports, and the questions on the first quiz, is it surprising the students didn't do better?

Although the learning tasks and the instructional approach were highly innovative, the first quiz was traditional in format and content. Why do you think the teacher used this test? What are the advantages and disadvantages of this format?

(Probe: how is math connected to the activities of the unit and the first quiz?)

The author expresses strong emotions: she is crushed. The quiz is the first benchmark by which she can judge the effectiveness of a new teaching approach. Many teachers have shared with us the deep disappointment they felt when an instructional innovation didn't work for them in the way developers promised it would. Have you had similar experiences? How did you feel? What did you do?

What were the students' feelings about the results of the quiz? One student said that he couldn't succeed on this quiz because he didn't know math. Do you agree?

There seems to be a great discrepancy between the results of this quiz and the teacher's perceptions about what students knew and were able to do. Have you found yourself in similar situations? What happened? What did you do?

The second quiz

Examine the second quiz carefully. In what ways is it different from the first? In what ways is it similar? To what extent does the second quiz have the potential to capture students' understanding of the concept of density better than the first?

The teacher proposes a number of explanations for why the students might have been more successful on the math portion of the second quiz than on the first. How do you assess her explanations? Do you have additional explanations the teacher didn't include?

How were the questions designed by students similar or different from questions on the first quiz? What do you think about students' suggestions? How can singing a song or writing a story reflect students' understanding of a scientific concept? How would you describe the difference between traditional and alternative assessment?

Assessment

This case prompted the teacher to reexamine her philosophy of assessment. In your opinion, what is the link between instruction and assessment? What should this link be? How can instruction and assessment be linked more closely?

Some teachers felt that when she developed the unit, the teacher should also have developed a different quiz that would reflect her goals for the unit. Do you agree?

What would this new test have looked like? In your opinion, do you have to redesign assessment each time you redesign a task or redesign the instruction?

The teacher planned to use various assessment tools: the individual reports, the quality of the group product, and the quiz. What kind of information about students' understanding can be gleaned from each type of assessment? How is the information from the various assessment tools complementary? Can information about students' learning from various assessment tools seem contradictory?

How are students' reports on their findings similar to a scientific convention? What specifically can a teacher find out about what students understand and are able to do at these scientific conventions?

In Complex Instruction, every student in the group completes an individual report at the end of each activity. Carefully examine the example of the individual report included in this case. How does completing such a report contribute to students' accountability as they work in groups? How does completion of individual reports stimulate substantive discussions about science?

The teacher also used the group products for assessment. To what extent is it important to evaluate the group as a whole (e.g., group process, group products)? What, if any, is the responsibility of the teacher in ensuring that the important information is included in group presentations? What would you do if students presented misinformation? (See Case 1.)

Some teachers were surprised that students in a high school science class would be asked to write journal entries. What kinds of information did the teacher gain from these journals? What is your opinion of the value of this information in general and for a high school science class in particular?

In this case, we don't know how the teacher responded to the journal entries. If your students were to write journal entries in your class, what would you do with them? How can journal entries be used for student assessment? For teacher self-assessment?

Interactions with colleagues

In a discussion with a colleague, the author commented that she noticed significant changes in her students. They seemed to appreciate the alternative test and the fact that they had taken part in the decision about how they were to be evaluated; they appeared more confident and were putting more effort into the course than they had previously. The colleague, however, had a less positive view. She felt that giving an alternative test was a disservice to the students, who would have to function and succeed in traditional settings in future. The author was exasperated. Have you ever found yourself in a similar situation? What did you do? What would you do if you were this author? What would your response be today if you were to find yourself in a similar situation? What would you say to a colleague? To a principal? To a parent? To a student?

Case 6

Struggles With the Dynamics of Grouping

The teacher in this case struggles with how to group children constructively and shares her strategies. The narrative follows one particular bilingual student, Sam, through three different groupings during the year. It describes what happens within each group and how the group dynamics appear to affect Sam's behavior. How to integrate English language learners into classroom activities, how groupwork can benefit or hinder such students, and how to evaluate student growth are among the questions this case raises.

CONTEXT

After teaching special education for 15 years in an inner-city school, this teacher decided to switch to regular education and was assigned a second grade class. She participates in the Fostering a Community of Learners (FCL) research project created by Ann Brown and Joe Campione at the University of California, Berkeley. FCL is an approach to groupwork in which deep disciplinary understanding and the development of skills of critical literacy are central. Students engage in collaborative research, then share their information and understandings through jigsaw and other activities, and finally apply what they have learned to a new and more difficult task that is reported in a public exhibition or performance. In an FCL classroom, groupwork activities elegantly synthesize several well-regarded approaches to groupwork, e.g., jigsaw (Aronson), reciprocal teaching (Palinscar and Brown), group investigation (Sharan), and writing process groups (National Writing Project).

QUESTIONS AND ISSUES

This teacher hoped groupwork would accomplish many things. What were her specific aims? How realistic were her expectations? What do you hope to accomplish with groupwork?

Why should we craft groups?

Unlike teachers who group children randomly or with little planning, this second grade teacher feels strongly that crafting groups in particular ways strongly influences how children learn. Yet no matter how hard a teacher tries, it's sometimes difficult to predict how the complex dynamics within groups will affect individual children. Why is this teacher so preoccupied with grouping? Note that she keeps students in groups for at least three weeks. This strategy may be different from the norm, where teachers group students for specific tasks that last no longer than three or four days.

How should we craft groups?

What is this teacher's philosophy of grouping? What were some of her strategies for placing children in groups? (Probe for stages of children's collaboration.) How do her strategies compare to the ways you group students? What are other strategies of grouping? What are the risks and benefits of each?

Sam's group experiences

What were some of the problems that arose in Sam's first group? What did the teacher do? What else might she have done? What are the risks and benefits of each suggested strategy? What would you have done in this situation? Why do you think Sam ended up at the bottom of the pecking order in his first group? What happened to Sam in subsequent groups? How do you account for the changes in group dynamics from the first group to the last?

The teacher was concerned about Sam's academic success relative to his interpersonal problems toward the end of the year. Some experts who read this case were not surprised at Sam's "attempt to wield power" in his group when his English skills improved. One commented, "That's not surprising. Wouldn't you do the same if no one ever listened to you?" What do you think?

Shifting the focus from Sam

Discussions often focus on how groups affected Sam's behavior, ignoring how Sam's participation affected other members of his groups. If discussion participants don't raise this issue, the leader should raise it to ensure that participants consider the case from multiple perspectives. Examine how Sam's presence affected the members of each of the groups he belonged to. How did the teacher handle each problem that arose? What alternate strategies might she have used? What are the risks and consequences of each?

The teacher alluded to other community-building activities she did with the class but didn't describe them. What might some of these activities be? What do you do to build community in your classroom?

Group effects on skills

Sam's verbal skills improved through groupwork. However, some of the teacher–author's colleagues felt that the emphasis on groupwork prevented Sam from developing independent reading and writing skills. What do you think?

Levels of interaction: Cooperation versus collaboration

In her depiction of the second group, the teacher initially described how the children worked cooperatively, though not collaboratively. It appears the group began to show evidence of collaboration during its work on the classic math story about Saint Ives. What's the difference between cooperation and collaboration? The author maintains that cooperation exists when students respect one another and do their jobs independently. A higher level of group interaction is collaboration, during which students work together on projects and share their thoughts. Examine the text for the teacher's account of Sam's second group. What's the difference between the two episodes? This teacher strives for evidence of both cooperation and collaboration during groupwork. As she stated in a personal communication to the editors, however, some groups never reach the collaborative mode. Think about the small groups you use or have observed. Do they show evidence of cooperation and collaboration? Give some specific examples.

How and when to intervene

Deciding whether or not to intervene while a group is working is one of the most difficult problems of groupwork. It is a theme that runs through most cases in this volume because it raises dilemmas that go to the heart of successful groupwork. These include delegating authority to students and respecting student teams and expecting them to make their own decisions. The teacher wonders whether and how to intervene on several occasions when she sees problems in Sam's groups. What actually happened in each situation? What did the teacher do? Are there other strategies she could have used? What problems might arise with each suggested strategy? What would/do you do in similar situations? What principles of teaching should you consider when making your decision?

Case 7

Puzzles of a Well-Crafted Group

This case highlights an English teacher's struggles in placing students in groups. The narrative describes his efforts to craft a group around an unusual student who, as a result of his background, "stands out" from the other students in an honors class. Despite the teacher's careful attempts to assemble a productive, supportive group, the students fail to collaborate, which results in a weak presentation to the class. What surprises and puzzles the teacher is that despite the group's inability to work together on the group presentation, each student's written essay reflects a solid understanding of the material studied during the group activity. The case provides opportunities to discuss the rationales teachers use to place students in groups and affords comparisons with Cases 3, 6, 9, 12, 15, and 16. A second issue for discussion is the range of groupwork tasks in the English classroom.

CONTEXT

This English teacher of six years' experience teaches in a suburban high school. It's the policy of his school's English department to track students. The author admits his "frustration" with this policy.

This teacher utilizes a process-oriented approach to writing instruction. That is, he places as much value on the process of generating written text as on the product of the final text. In process-oriented writing classrooms, the teacher devotes attention to helping students understand the unique and recursive nature of writing by introducing the various components of the writing process—for example, generating and organizing ideas, composing a draft, soliciting responses, and making revisions based on responses. In this class the teacher has his students meet regularly in writing response groups to share and critique drafts of assignments before they are submitted to him. The teacher prepares students to work in writing response groups by modeling helpful feedback and having the class generate criteria for response.

QUESTIONS AND ISSUES

The teacher acknowledges his puzzlement, and even ambivalence, over how to craft productive groups, taking "some careful thought" to "assemble a group around Daryl." What are his concerns about Daryl? What rationales or "precepts for group construction" does he offer for the selection of each member of the group formed around Daryl? How has the English department's policy of tracking been factored into the teacher's decision making? After the activity, how does the teacher reevaluate those precepts? What do you think of his "precepts for group construction"? How do they compare to the precepts you use when you form groups?

Daryl

How does the teacher describe Daryl? In what ways does the teacher feel Daryl stands out? How do you think the other students perceived Daryl? How do you think Daryl feels in this class?

The groupwork task

What are the specific requirements of the assignment? What are the teacher's instructional goals, and how does he reevaluate them after the activity is completed? The teacher had placed the students in writing response groups for five to six weeks prior to this groupwork project. Writing response groups do not typically require the same degree of interdependence that well-designed groupwork tasks do. How had the students' work in a writing response group prepared them for the requirements of this first extended project?

Reaching consensus

The task requires that students reach consensus over which poem they want to present and teach to the class. In your opinion, why does the group struggle to reach consensus? How significant a role did the actual poems in the anthology play in the group's struggle to reach consensus?

The teacher describes his "increasing disappointment" as he observes Daryl's group's attempt to reach consensus. In vivid detail he captures their body language and conversation. How do you think each student felt? What is your analysis of the group's problem in reaching consensus? The course to take when a group is having group process problems can be less obvious than when a group is clearly laboring under content-related misconceptions. Sometimes we hesitate to step in because we don't know how to help them cooperate or because we hope students will work things out. How does the teacher respond to the group's struggles? What might the teacher have done to help the students learn how to reach consensus? What strategies do you use to teach students how to reach consensus?

Should consensus always be the aim in groupwork? What room is there for respectful disagreement, rather than consensus? What do you think might have happened if the task had not required consensus?

The teacher remarks that the group had "worked together off and on for five to six weeks, primarily in writing response groups." How do the interactions required for writing response prepare students for the give-and-take of reaching consensus?

The written paragraphs

The high quality of the students' written analyses of the poem "Gravy" surprises the teacher. Why do you think he is surprised? How do you account for the students' success on this part of the assignment? What relation do you see between the written paragraph and other parts of the assignment?

Student evaluations of the activity

The teacher asks each student to evaluate his or her contribution during the groupwork activity. He describes the written response required of each student. What does he learn from these evaluations? How do you think this information helped shape his reflections on this lesson? What are other strategies for student evaluation? What are the risks and benefits of each?

Case 8

My Struggle With Sharon

Students who tend to be bossy and disruptive during group activities are the focus of this case. The teacher attempts to craft a group capable of cooperating with a student she perceives as difficult and completing a rather complex activity. However, the difficult student, Sharon, disrupts the group from the very beginning. When Sharon and another group member, Alicia, each independently ask to leave the group, the teacher assigns Alicia to another group and leaves Sharon and the others to fend for themselves. Though Sharon's group is able to complete its assignment and present it to the class, the teacher questions her handling of the episode.

CONTEXT

This case is from an ethnically diverse school which is 60% Hispanic and 25% Caucasian. The remaining 15% of students are African American, Pacific Islander, and Middle Eastern. In this particular eighth grade language arts classroom, twelve of the 24 students are labeled "Resource Special Education" pupils.

QUESTIONS AND ISSUES

There are several reasons why groups fall apart. One is students who either are disruptive or don't share in the task (see other cases in this section). But often, when we analyze what happened from different perspectives, we find other explanations that are not so apparent. Let's look at this case from several lenses.

One explanation for group failure that rarely receives enough attention is the nature and purpose of the group task itself. As a teacher in one of our sessions said, "Groupwork has become such a fad, we often don't think carefully enough about why we use it in our classroom." Look closely at the nature of the task in this case. What was the teacher's purpose for her unit? Was groupwork the best way for her to achieve its purpose? What are the advantages? What are the drawbacks? What did the teacher hope to gain from putting students in groups for this task? What might she have to

lose? In general, what do/should you consider when you use groupwork in your classroom? What do you hope to gain from these activities?

In planning this unit, the teacher noted that while students had previously worked on numerous group projects, none was "so encompassing." This project certainly differed from what she had done in prior years, when students wrote down their stories individually and each sought peer response from another student. Do you think the task the teacher designed is a challenging one? What would make it challenging? How might a group think about how to tackle this task? What decisions are required? How can students be helped to learn decision making processes? (See the discussion of reaching consensus for Case 7.)

Crafting a group

This teacher took grouping seriously. As she planned her unit, she carefully placed students in groups taking into consideration their abilities, skills, and personalities. When half the class was absent, she recrafted groups according to students' achievement levels—high, medium, low, and nonachievers. Sharon, Roy, Alicia, and Charles were each described according to one of these achievement levels. Look at the teacher's description of each of these students. Describe each student using the teacher's language. What do you think of the descriptions she used of "low achiever" and "nonachiever"? What do you think of the criteria she initially used to group students? How do those criteria compare to the ones she used for the second set of groups? Other teachers who've read this case have wondered what the teacher did when the 12 absent students returned to class the following day. What would you do?

In retrospect, the teacher questions her strategy of grouping and suggests she might not in future place Sharon with other strong personalities like Alicia; she hopes Sharon will "learn to cooperate with all students, not just the ones who follow her." What are the implications of this strategy for Sharon and the other students in the class? What would/do you consider when you place potentially uncooperative students in groups?

At the end of the narrative, the teacher raises a question related to the notion of grouping. She asks, "Should I form groups by lottery and not try to make all groups equal in abilities and skills?" What do you think of random grouping?

Roles in groupwork

Like the teachers in Cases 3 and 10, this teacher assigns a procedural role to each student to help him or her take responsibility for keeping the group on task and working productively. These roles, which include facilitator, reporter, recorder, and gatherer/harmonizer, are designed to free the teacher from the burden of management. If students take responsibility for directions and materials, for example, it makes it possible for teachers to attend to students' thinking and learning.

What was the teacher thinking when she gave the role of reporter to Sharon and the role of facilitator to Alicia? How do you think each girl perceived the reasons for her assignment? How might other group members have viewed these assignments?

What do you consider to be the value of roles? Are there any drawbacks? What might have happened in the group in this case if there had been no roles? What might have happened if the roles had been assigned differently?

The teacher's knowledge of Sharon and Alicia

How does the teacher describe each girl? Why might Sharon act the way she does? How do you think the girls regard each other? How do the other students regard each of them? How do you think the teacher feels about the two girls? How do you think they feel about the teacher?

Intervening in a dysfunctional group

As many of the other cases in this volume illustrate, intervening constructively is one of the most common problems in groupwork; it is no different here. Look closely at what happened to students in group 3 soon after the students were assigned to their groups. What was the teacher's intervention strategy when she saw trouble brewing? Why did she talk only to Alicia? What were the ramifications of this strategy for Sharon and the others? Some teachers feel that this tactic was demeaning to Sharon. What do you think? What evidence is there for this interpretation?

At the end of the narrative, the teacher wonders, "Was I wrong in encouraging Alicia to cooperate instead of focusing on Sharon and encouraging her to be more cooperative?" She also notes that "Even nonachievers like Sharon want to be successful." How might the teacher have been more helpful with Sharon? What are the risks and benefits of each strategy?

Allowing students to leave a group

There are often kids who want to leave a group in which they're not happy. Some teachers don't force the issue and allow students to work alone if they choose to. Others feel it is important for students to learn how to get along with everyone and insist that individuals solve their personal problems (see Case 9). In this case, however, the teacher gave mixed messages. When Sharon and Alicia independently asked to leave the group, she refused Sharon's request but acquiesced to Alicia's. What were the ramifications? For Sharon? For Alicia? For the rest of the group? What might have happened if the teacher had not moved Alicia? What would you have done?

Assessment

Using appropriate assessment is one of the most critical factors in successful groupwork. In this case the teacher gave the group project a common grade, part of which was based on cooperation. What do you think of this grading system? Is it fair to give each group member the same grade, regardless of the amount of work he or she put in? Some educators think that there should be two grades for each group project—a group grade and an individual grade. As you think about assessment for groupwork, what should you consider?

At the end of the narrative, the teacher raises the following question: "How can I distinguish successful student growth in this particular project if I allow students to move to other groups when they encounter problems?" How would you respond to her question?

Incentives for groupwork

As Alicia said to the teacher after making her presentation with her new group, "It was easier to work with a group that wanted the story to look good and sound good. I liked working with a group that found positive, fun solutions." Anyone who has experience as a group member knows that Alicia is correct. And no matter how committed to groupwork one is, an experience in a dysfunctional group can be very sobering. For high-achieving students like Alicia, what are the incentives to work with others who may not have the same standards she has (see Case 16)? What are some general principles teachers can use when students have different standards of achievement?

My struggle with Sharon

How do you interpret the title of the case? What is the nature of this teacher's struggle? How do you explain her struggle? Have you ever had struggles with a particular student? What did you do? As you reflect on this case, might you do anything different?

Case 9

To Be, or "Not"

This case revolves around two students who can't get along with each other. The teacher avoids putting them in the same group; but one day, when he is too preoccupied to notice, the luck of the draw puts them together. Disaster strikes. Their quarreling leads the teacher to stop the group. He asks the group to come up with a plan for how the two students can work together, and they do. The teacher reflects on what caused the conflict and reports on conversations with both students, so we are provided multiple perspectives on the situation. The teacher also shares his beliefs about how students need to learn to work with anyone, even if they say, "Not him!" or "Not her!"

CONTEXT

This is an eighth grade physical science class at a middle school in a large California city. Most students come from the surrounding middle-class neighborhood; the rest are bused from other areas of the city. The teacher is a male in his fourth year of teaching who sees himself teaching "kids, not subjects," and who places considerable emphasis on social skills, problem solving, and decision making.

QUESTIONS AND ISSUES

This case is written in two parts. The first section ends with the group arguing and the teacher saying to himself, "What was I to do?" One way to handle the case discussion is to do it in two stages, giving the group only part I and asking them what they would do. This focuses their attention explicitly on solving the immediate management problem and lets them suggest a variety of intervention approaches before they read (and discuss) what this teacher actually did. What can a teacher do at this point? What are the risks and benefits to different approaches? What are some signs teachers use to determine when and how to step in?

After reading the second section, participants can respond to the intervention that the teacher chooses. Notice that the teacher places the responsibility for

solving the problem on the group. What are the benefits and risks of this approach? What experience have teachers had with this kind of approach? How can it be structured to work successfully? Some teachers have commented, for instance, that they would never send students out of the room alone. Is this an issue? Some people feel that the ending is too rosy. They believe that it worked out well because Caroline and Dennis are highly motivated students. What evidence is there for this interpretation? Do you think it would have worked out differently in another setting?

What difference would it make if no safety factors were involved? Would that allow the teacher to wait longer, or to intervene in a different way? Is it ever appropriate to let a group fail?

Some teachers feel there was a "self-fulfilling prophecy" operating here, that the teacher expected the students not to get along (hence the "I told you so" voice in his head). Do you think his expectations led him to intervene too soon? Did his expectations influence the way he intervened?

Why is the group dysfunctional?

We can all relate to the general situation raised in this case—a dysfunctional group. Teachers are always concerned about this and sometimes ask why certain groups fall apart—those we predict and those we don't. This case offers us a chance to do some detective work about this particular problem. The author focuses on the personalities of these two students as the source of conflict (see, for instance, his concluding paragraphs). But the case as a whole offers a number of clues, including the comments of the two students. Why did this group function so poorly?

Preparation. What training did the students have for working in groups? The writer said that social skills were a "frequent topic of conversation" in the classroom, but he did not mention any particular training in group skills. When the group fell apart, he assigned a "social skills activity" of coming up with an action plan for completing the lab. Do you suppose that "developing a plan" was a regular part of their approach to groupwork? How can students be prepared to work in groups?

Was the task appropriate? How did the nature of the lab activity contribute to the situation? Caroline felt that their problems were exacerbated in the group because everyone wanted to get involved, but there wasn't enough material for everyone to have something to do. Comment on her observation. Each student had to complete an individual report, but there was no group product, no group accountability. What difference might this have made?

Dennis suggested that the task should be structured to "give everyone a specific job." What about this idea? He went on to define this as "allowing each person to participate without interference from the others." Was a group task designated in this situation? Why were students working in a group?

"Control freaks." Dennis uses the term "control freaks" to describe himself and Caroline. Most teachers will readily relate to this description. What experiences have you had with students who like to be in charge? How have you dealt with such students, who often have a difficult time with groupwork? Compare this situation to the one in Case 15. Some sociologists would describe this as a conflict between two high-status students. How might it be useful to analyze the situation in these terms?

Gender issues. To middle school teachers, it may be no surprise that this conflict is between a boy and a girl. Students at this age are often intensely interested in members of the opposite sex and in working out issues of peer relationships. The teacher considers the possibility that this is a "love–hate relationship." Do you think gender was a significant factor in this situation? If so, what difference would that make in how the teacher might handle the situation? Would it have been different with two girls or with two boys?

Crafting groups

One issue raised by this case is how a teacher assigns students to groups. This teacher believes in random assignment. What are the advantages and disadvantages of this approach? The teacher believes that students need to learn to work with anybody and that random assignment accomplishes this. Do you agree?

"Nots"

The writer uses the term "nots" to refer to students with whom others don't want to work. This concept often sparks recognition and discussion among teachers. Dennis and Carolyn are "nots" to each other, but they aren't really typical of the sort of student no one wants to work with. Typically, "nots" are students who are generally unpopular; often they are low achievers and are avoided or teased by others. What experience have you had with students who are "nots"? What were these students like? What strategies did you use to increase their acceptance and participation?

Case 10

Confronting One Group's Inertia

After completing a summer workshop on collaborative groupwork, this veteran teacher had high hopes for how groupwork would benefit her freshman reading class of low achievers. But one dysfunctional group of boys struggled and had nothing to show for their final presentation to the class. Instead, they admitted that they hadn't been very serious about the assignment. Though the teacher used this experience to explore responses to uncooperative group members in her class, she wondered what effect this experience had on the boys involved. This case provides rich opportunities to discuss introducing a class to groupwork and working with dysfunctional groups. It raises many of the same issues as Case 4, "Do You Let Kids Fail?"

CONTEXT

The students in this freshman reading class were primarily African American and had reading scores between grade levels 4.0 and 6.8. Approximately 75% of the students in this class were bused daily from a community 15 miles away. According to the teacher, most of the students had trouble competing academically with other students and were "burdened with feelings of inferiority."

QUESTIONS AND ISSUES

What did this teacher hope to accomplish from groupwork? What did she expect would happen? What actually happened?

Examining the task

This teacher's introductory groupwork task involved a set of activities designed to examine the poetic form of a given poem. As she stated in her case, the main purpose of the task was to help students develop cooperative learning skills, not to foster expertise in poetic verse. Several teachers have raised questions about the selection of this particular task for groupwork. Was it interesting and compelling enough to engage the students? Could students relate to the poetry discussed in class, let alone the particular poems assigned to their groups? Was the task at the appropriate level of difficulty for these students? These are important questions to discuss, because the success of groupwork often rests on the nature of the task. If we expect students to work cooperatively and collaboratively in small group settings, we must carefully design tasks that are intrinsically interesting, compelling, and at an appropriate level of difficulty. They must also require a contribution from all group members. Are there other criteria for selecting group tasks you would add? Given these criteria, what kinds of activities would you choose for groupwork?

Introducing the task

This teacher spent a lot of time introducing the task. What exactly did she do? (Probe for details about introducing the content of the lesson *and* group skillbuilders.) Would you add any other activities? As she said in the case, the trust-building activities set the stage for exchange by diminishing the students' fears of being laughed at. Do you agree that these introductory activities are enough to diminish the students' fear? What's reasonable to expect from this first group activity?

If the teacher had consciously or unconsciously communicated to the students that she was interested more in developing their cooperative learning skills than in improving their expertise in poetic form, might this communicate to the students that the task itself wasn't really that important? How might this influence the students' desire to complete a given task?

Crafting groups

The teacher selected group members arbitrarily, which resulted in one group consisting of four boys with low reading skills. At the end of the case, the teacher noted that in the future, she would assert more control over grouping students heterogeneously. Assigning students to groups is a theme that several teacher–authors discuss in their cases. Do you purposefully craft groups? If yes, what criteria do you use for grouping students? Are there any advantages in grouping students randomly?

What do we know about the group?

What happened when the four boys discovered they were in a group together? The teacher inferred from their behavior that the boys didn't care if the group worked together. Do you agree? Why do you think they responded as they did? Is it possible that the facilitator had trouble reading and feared being embarrassed in front of his peers? The tic-tac-toe players asked to be placed in another group, but the teacher refused. What might this tell you about these boys' desire to finish the task? Could this be a clue that they really wanted to achieve some success?

It's often easy to cover up reading difficulties and other inadequacies in large group settings. But in small groups, where each member is required to make a contribution, it is much harder to hide these inadequacies. Given their history of academic failure, what did these boys have to risk in small group settings? What can you do to alleviate such a situation?

Roles and responsibilities

Though the teacher didn't elaborate on how she used roles for managing each group, we can infer that she assigned specific roles to each group member. A list of duties for each role was on the board. What were some of the designated roles and responsibilities? Why didn't the roles work in this situation? What might have happened if there were no designated roles? Are there any disadvantages or limitations to using roles? What alternative strategies might you use? What possible problems can happen with each one?

How and when should a teacher intervene?

When it became clear that this group had difficulty beginning its task, the teacher was uncomfortable and walked over to facilitate. But when asked how to get started, she resisted the temptation to provide substan-

tive help; she feared it would discourage independent learning. How and when to intervene is a common theme in these cases. If you really want to delegate the responsibility for learning to students, you have to encourage them to look to one another for help. But what is the teacher's responsibility if no one in the group understands what is required? Do you think these students really didn't understand the task, or were their questions a ploy to resist getting started? How can you find out?

This teacher let the group flounder for a couple of days, optimistically hoping that the students would begin to work on their own. But the group never coalesced and had nothing prepared for their final presentation to the class. Examine the teacher's intervention strategies on both days of the lesson. How would you evaluate her strategies? What are some alternative strategies she could have used? What are the risks and benefits of each?

Do you have similar situations in your classroom? What things do you consider when deciding whether and how to intervene in small groups? Given the discussion today, other case discussions, and your previous experience, how would you make your decisions? Give some examples.

Impact on students

Though the teacher used the group's dysfunctional experience as a learning opportunity for the whole class and felt that the discussion had some benefits, she questioned the impact on the four students involved. "If the effect [on students] was negative, were the merits of groupwork undermined?" The teacher in Case 5 had a similar dilemma and asked, "Should we allow kids to fail?" How would you respond to these questions?

Case 11

Silences: The Case of the Invisible Boy

This case offers excellent opportunities to explore helping low-status students in small group settings. The veteran middle school teacher uses new groupwork strategies she learned over the summer to help with a low-achieving student but finds it is much more difficult than she had anticipated. Though the student probably participates more in small group tasks than he would in a traditional setting, he makes no "miraculous academic recovery." More sobered by experience at the end of the year than at the beginning, the teacher reflects on what happened and comes to some painful conclusions.

CONTEXT

Working in an inner-city middle school with a predominantly African American student body, this teacher struggles to motivate her low-achieving students. The class is an eighth grade core of combined language arts and social studies. This year she pins her hopes on Complex Instruction, a program she learned in a seminar.

QUESTIONS AND ISSUES

Look closely at the case. What specifically does this teacher hope to gain from Complex Instruction? (Probe for the ideas that low achievers improve academically as a result of participating in groupwork and student learning increases in proportion to student interaction.) Why would the teacher believe this? What evidence supports her beliefs?

Multiple perceptions about Dennis

What details does the teacher use to describe Dennis? (Probe for examples: membership in B-Boys; artistic ability; poor academic record as compared with average test scores; low reading and writing skills; reputation among students as being weak intellectually; expertise at being disengaged and making himself invisible; and predilection for giving the standard answer, "I don't know," when asked a question.) What might she think of him?

What is your analysis of Dennis's problem? What evidence do you draw from the narrative? Some teachers have suggested that he could be a passive resister—someone who uses power to manipulate a group to do his work. Others wondered, since he was a gang member, if it might be "uncool" to be a good student. What do you think? What are the advantages of using groupwork with Dennis? Are there any disadvantages?

Let's take a moment to imagine Dennis's experience in this class. From his perspective, what does he think about the class? Include in your conjecture what he thinks about groupwork, the teacher, and the other students.

Status issues

Some teachers speculated about the issues of power that are involved in status interventions. They wondered what risks there are to the learning community (classroom) if they set themselves up to confer status on students. Do you agree? What are some other ways to provide status intervention? What are the short-term and long-term consequences of your ideas?

Intervention strategies

This teacher poignantly describes her struggle finding opportunities to "assign competence" to Dennis (publicly recognize his contributions). It was much harder than she had anticipated. As she stated in the case, he rarely did anything that warranted recognition. Waiting for an opportunity to provide such recognition is a common problem for teachers with low-status students (see other cases in this section). Teachers know the importance of providing status interventions and are frustrated when they find few appropriate occasions.

Early in the year. What intervention strategies did the teacher actually use with Dennis? (Probe for strategies like conferencing with him and with other students, grouping him with supportive students, and assigning tasks that required artistic ability.) Can you suggest other tactics? What are the risks and benefits of each?

Were there any missed opportunities that merited public recognition? Some have suggested that the teacher missed an opportunity by not drawing attention to the metaphor of the tricycle Dennis had drawn in November. How might she have used it?

Some teachers were concerned about the kids who ended up in Dennis's group and wondered how to support them. What do the other kids think about Dennis? How difficult is it for some group members when kids like Dennis don't appear to be contributing their share to an assigned task? What strategies can you recommend for supporting Dennis's group members? What are the trade-offs for each?

Audiotaped group meeting. In April, the teacher audiotaped a small group session to see if she could understand why Dennis hadn't flourished under her "tutelage and Complex Instruction." What happened during this session? What did the teacher do when she saw that Dennis wasn't engaged in the group task? What was the reaction of the other group members? When the teacher asked how they were making Dennis feel a part of their group, Dennis replied, "I helped answer the questions." Later he explained, "They're letting me discuss Carroll. They're talking about how she lived and stuff." How did the teacher interpret these comments? How do you interpret them? Was he engaged in the task? Did he contribute?

Silences

Several teachers have questioned the term "silences." Who is silent? Is it only Dennis? What about the teacher? Aren't the students in Dennis's groups also silent about his participation in group activities? Why is everyone pretending that Dennis is contributing? Did the class perceive that they had to protect Dennis for some reason?

After listening to the tape several times, the teacher had to admit to herself that Dennis never contributed to the group's discussion. What is the impact on the group when one person remains silent? How much can you expect from Carmen and Tiffany, who worked on the task? How responsible should they be for Dennis's contribution? What about Tonesha? She also didn't appear to contribute.

What did the teacher learn about her perceived collaboration with Dennis's silence? Do you agree with her assessment of the situation? The teacher said that she was concerned about being too confrontational with Dennis for fear he would "close down even further." What might have happened if the teacher had been more demanding? What would/do you do in your classroom with students like Dennis?

Assessment

One of the most important criterion of successful groupwork is accountability—both individual and group. Some teachers wondered how the teacher graded students and whether she could have provided an alternate way of assessing Dennis. What do you think? The teacher–author doesn't mention how she assessed her students. But as you think about your own classroom, how would you hold students accountable for their efforts? What kind of assessments would you use?

Realistic expectations

Many teachers wondered whether the case author was too hard on herself when she determined that she was a partner in Dennis's silence. Do you agree? What's realistic to expect from an inner-city middle school teacher with 36 kids in her class?

Cooperative magic?

This teacher realizes that there is no "cooperative magic" either in Complex Instruction or in groupwork in general (see Case 6). She believes that these models of teaching offer increased opportunities for academic participation and can be positive experiences for the participants, but they do not "turn every kid into an 'A' student." Do you agree with her assessment? What generalizations can you make about groupwork? What kind of roles and responsibilities to make groupwork successful should teachers assume?

Case 12

Learning to Listen to Robert

The teacher in this case explores her belief that "low-status children can drive classroom conversations in new and exciting directions." These beliefs are tested by Robert, a child who has severe speech and communication problems but is capable of deep ideas about science content. The teacher describes her early observations of Robert and a time when she intervened in the group, leading them to listen to his ideas about science. While the episode was successful and her belief was confirmed, the teacher notes that there was "limited transfer"—his group still ignored Robert. The teacher struggles with conflicting priorities; she sees her intervention as a way to "level the playing field so that all students can participate fully" and benefit from each other's ideas. But she wonders how much intervention is needed and how she can capture the best opportunities and thereby limit her interference with students' ownership of their learning.

CONTEXT

This case is authored by a twelve-year veteran teacher of elementary school science. She teaches a combination fifth/sixth grade science class in an urban elementary school with a large minority population. This is her fourth year with the Brown/Campione project, Fostering a Community of Learners (FCL). FCL is an approach to groupwork in which deep disciplinary understanding and the development of skills of critical literacy are central. Students engage in collaborative research, then share their information and understandings through jigsaw and other activities, and finally apply what they have learned to a new and more difficult task that is reported in a public exhibition or performance. In an FCL classroom, groupwork activities elegantly synthesize several well-regarded approaches to groupwork, e.g., jigsaw (Aronson), reciprocal teaching (Palinscar and Brown), group investigation (Sharan), and writing process groups (National Writing Project).

QUESTIONS AND ISSUES

Participants in a case discussion are likely to feel concern for Robert. They may wonder about the nature of his communicative disorder and want to know what resources are available in the school or community to help him. They may suggest strategies for addressing his specific problem.

Robert's role

In the end, this case is not about just Robert, but about his role in the group. He has a lot to share, but because of his dysfunctional speech patterns, his group ignores him. What can be done to help the group learn to listen to him?

What is the activity structure in FCL? To what extent does it create group interdependence by giving everyone something to contribute? How does it structure students' interaction? To what extent do these things "level the playing field"? What would make this work more effectively? What's missing?

Modes of communication

Notice the heavy emphasis on talking in this class. Should there be other ways to present besides orally? Robert seems to be a skilled artist. His science diagrams are insightful. Can this mode of communication be made more prominent in the class or more necessary to group tasks? How? Would this make a difference? Could the teacher "assign competence" to Robert? What might she say?

The teacher notes that students negotiated deep meaning only "after the discussion had slowed down enough so that children actually listened to each other." Could this be a problem that goes beyond Robert? How can students learn to listen to each other and develop ideas more fully? How can these skills be taught?

Teacher intervention

The teacher sees her own skilled and timely intervention as an important tool in changing the group process and deepening the discussion, yet she is keenly aware of the cost of her intervention. It shifts control of the group, at least temporarily, from students to teacher, detracting from her goal of having students take maximal ownership of their learning. This theme comes up in a number of cases (see Case 1). What experience have people had with this dilemma? When is it appropriate to intervene?

The teacher observed Robert for some time and noticed an opportunity that she had missed (the DDT discussion) before she was ready to seize an opportunity to intervene. How can teachers be prepared? What techniques have people used to help themselves notice and remember what's going on during groupwork?

Is it surprising the teacher's intervention had little long-term effect on the group? Should she have intervened more? What is the teacher's responsibility to individual students? How much time do you take for one student in a class of 30?

Case 13

The Chance I Had Been Waiting For

The teacher in this case is experienced in groupwork and specifically in using Complex Instruction. She believes cooperative groups are effective at helping students build abilities such as "reading and writing, balancing, building, drawing, estimating, hypothesizing, and measuring." She also seems to believe cooperative learning is somewhat magical—that students can interact regardless of their language ability, develop a sense of belonging, become active participants, and build their self-esteem. Given this teacher's beliefs and her previous successful experiences, she was surprised when Miguel, a low-status student, joined her class and "cooperative learning was not helping him at all."

The teacher watched carefully for opportunities to identify Miguel's strengths. In May the teacher noticed a significant incident as he was working with his group. Unlike his groupmates, he was able to build a sturdy structure by following a diagram. The teacher gave him specific, positive, and public feedback (she assigned competence to him) and pointed out to the group that Miguel knew what to do and could serve as a resource for them. This intervention made a difference in Miguel's subsequent interactions with his classmates.

CONTEXT

The setting for this case is a bilingual classroom. Like many of her students, the teacher is originally from Mexico. She relates with sensitivity to the struggles of her Spanish-speaking and English-learning students. The teacher utilizes Complex Instruction and has added a special role—that of a translator—to each group.

QUESTIONS AND ISSUES

The teacher identifies the conditions that make for successful groupwork: tasks need to be rich and complex so students can learn from one another; students should learn by doing; and teachers should facilitate learning instead of imparting information. The teacher has successfully encouraged students to use their intellectual abilities, and she publicly recognizes

them for doing so. In many ways, this teacher has had significant positive experiences. Although she questions whether and when to intervene and how to equalize participation in groups, groupwork runs quite smoothly in her classroom.

What are some of the necessary conditions for successful groupwork that this teacher talks about? How does the fact that she is an immigrant help her better understand her students? How, if at all, can students interact in groups regardless of their language proficiency? How can they learn from each other if they do not speak the same language? How does groupwork develop a sense of belonging? Increase students' self-concept?

Miguel, a low-status student

Miguel, a third grader who didn't seem to become integrated into the classroom, is described by the teacher as "shy and withdrawn." These are often code words for low-status students. Many teachers use them to describe students who rarely, if ever, participate in groupwork, who are perceived as slow, and who have few friends. These words place the burden of low status on the students—if only they learned how to speak up, if only they were more friendly, if only they tried harder, if only they participated more.

Have you known students like Miguel? How did they behave in the classroom? How did other students perceive them? How did you? Why do many students like Miguel become behavior problems? How did Miguel's home situation contribute to his difficulties in school?

The teacher clearly recognizes the group's culpability in Miguel's situation: "When I observed Miguel's group I saw that the other members simply wouldn't give him a chance." What is the relationship between Miguel's shyness and the group's unwillingness to give him a chance? How can students become more aware of the consequences of their behavior in groups? What are the consequences of Miguel's low status as far as group process is concerned?

It is important to realize that when grading for participation in groups, teachers often forget that some students don't participate because groups won't give them a chance. How would you evaluate and grade Miguel's participation in the group?

The teacher's intervention

What did Miguel do well? How was what he did an intellectually resourceful problem solving activity? What did the teacher's intervention consist of? Why did she make the analogy to the architect's work? Some teachers who have read the case argued that architects don't "build structures by following diagrams." What do you think? Why was it important that the group hear what Miguel had to say?

Was the teacher guilty of making "much ado about nothing"? Was her feedback out of proportion? What would you have said? What could Miguel have been thinking? What might his groupmates have been thinking?

What were the consequences of the teacher's intervention for Miguel? For his classmates? For the teacher herself? Some teachers were worried that the teacher's positive feedback to Miguel would detract from the status of the other students. How do you feel about that?

Note. Research shows that these types of intervention strategies do not decrease the level of participation of high-status students.

It's never enough

In spite of her successful intervention, the teacher felt she hadn't done enough. If only she had paid more and better attention to Miguel! Paying attention and carefully observing students, particularly low-status stu-dents, is an important first step for a successful intervention. How can we ensure that we have the opportunity to do this?

Many teachers identified with the teacher's sense of guilt over not having done enough for Miguel. What do you think? If you had a student like Miguel, what else could you do to make him participate more in groups? To have his groupmates pay more attention to him? How could the teacher have created further opportunities for Miguel to be successful? How will his success in groups contribute to his increased success in academic tasks?

Note. This case is best used as a companion activity to Elizabeth Cohen's video *Status Treatments in the Classroom* (see references in the introduction of the casebook). Watching the video, we get to know Miguel as well as the teacher. The additional information provided in the case further helps to illustrate the context for the assigning competence treatment used in Complex Instruction. What matters in this case is not only the intervention itself (where the teacher explains to the group that Miguel's contribution is important to the group), but the fact that we actually see a student walk up to Miguel and talk to him immediately following the intervention.

Many Complex Instruction teachers identified with the case writer. On one hand, they felt she belabored the point and overreacted to a small incident. On the other, they shared her sense of guilt about the fact that it wasn't until May, at almost the end of the academic year, that she was able to see something Miguel contributed to his group.

Case 14

_____

An Extra Audience of Critics: Handling a Parent's Response

One of the political challenges facing teachers is to persuade parents that groupwork, particularly multiple-ability groupwork, is a beneficial instructional strategy. Frequently parents are not aware of or do not understand the rationale underlying groupwork in general, and the use of open-ended learning activities that include many different intellectual abilities (in addition to the traditional academic abilities of reading and writing) in particular. When this happens, the stage is set for a potential conflict between parents, who are worried about their children's academic advancement, and teachers, who have come to appreciate the benefits of groupwork.

CONTEXT

The author of this case is an intern teacher who, unlike most student teachers, has sole responsibility for a classroom. She is supervised by a cooperating teacher from the school site and a supervisor from the university. The author teaches in an upscale suburb in the San Francisco Bay Area, where many parents are college educated. They are involved in and vocal about how things should or shouldn't be run in the schools. While the teacher has few discipline problems and most of her students are highly motivated to succeed academically, this seemingly enviable setting is a mixed blessing: parent interest and involvement can be supportive, but the "extra audience of critics" can be particularly intimidating for a teacher new to the profession.

QUESTIONS AND ISSUES

The learning task described in this case is the culminating activity of a unit on the Renaissance. While focusing on the distinction between the Renaissance and the Middle Ages, students were expected to draw connections between Renaissance art and the major intellectual themes of the period. In that sense this unit seems to be an excellent humanities activity.

What was the teacher's rationale for her unit? What were her goals? Given the "big idea" of the unit, to what extent was it a natural fit for an interdisciplinary take on the Renaissance? What is the role of art education in this learning task?

How well did the teacher plan ahead? How well did she lay out the different components of the unit: content, process, and assessment?

Was the task a high-level, intellectually challenging task, or might the parent have been right—saying that it was just "fluff" and "crap"?

Assessment

The teacher feels that by a variety of criteria and measures (a test, essays, performances in class, high student engagement throughout the process, and peer grading), she had achieved her goal and the unit was a resounding success. The cooperating teacher and the department chair were "impressed with the complexity of the reports and the pride that the students took in posing."

What do you think about these criteria and measures for evaluating student learning? How well did the teacher achieve her goals? (Probe for the response that students made impressive connections between the paintings and general Renaissance themes.) Was there adequate balance between individual assessment and group assessment? How successful was the teacher in holding students accountable, both as individuals and as members of a group? What would you consider adequate measures of success for this unit?

Given the overall positive outcomes, why would a single letter from one parent have such a devastating effect on this teacher? Why couldn't she respond in a more balanced way? How could she have used her assessment measures to convince the parent about the positive outcomes of the unit? In general, how could assessment outcomes serve as a political tool to legitimize innovative instructional approaches?

Differing perceptions of teaching and learning

We can assume from the description of the setting that the letter-writing parent is well educated and perhaps holds an advanced degree. How might this parent's previous educational experience affect his perceptions of teaching and learning? Why would he be so concerned about time in the school having been spent on seemingly frivolous activities? What might be his view of the various disciplines? (Probe for the response that algebra is the "real stuff.") He talks about another instance when he wrote a letter to a teacher. What could that letter have been about?

What are the costs and benefits of an involved and well-educated parent group? How might the teacher's and the parents' (many of whom have advanced degrees) conceptions of what teaching and learning are about differ? What might be the consequences of these differences?

How could the teacher have prepared the parents for her planned departure from traditional learning tasks and activities? To what extent was such preparation her responsibility? An option? Should the administration—the principal, department head, and cooperating teacher—have known about this innovative project in advance?

How might this parent and other parents be persuaded that art education is an important part of social studies or a humanities curriculum? How could the teacher justify having spent so much time on an activity, given the time pressures of content coverage in high schools?

The parent's letter and the teacher's response

The parent's letter is rude, patronizing, and from the teacher's point of view, infuriating. The parent uses insulting language, from "hokey" to "crap" and "fluff." Such language demeans the teacher's ideas on effective teaching and learning. The parent considers the task entertainment, not serious learning.

How would you feel if you received a letter like this? Why does one letter have so much power over this teacher? Often parents write letters to complain or protest. How often do they write letters to commend a teacher on a particularly successful assignment—a job well done? What are the consequences of such parent behavior for teachers' professional satisfaction and self-efficacy?

How might Sara have felt about her father's letter? What might her role have been in this incident? In your opinion, did Sara share her father's feelings? Why did the teacher feel the need to reevaluate her relationship with Sara? Could she have thought that Sara had misrepresented the assignment?

The teacher responded with a short note. What do you think about her response? Are you satisfied with her letter? Did it give you a sense of closure? What would you have written? You might want to jot down an outline for such a reply or practice a response to a parent who criticizes similar work in your classroom. This case discussion could provide a good opportunity to prepare and rehearse arguments defending a teacher's choice of such an activity or groupwork in general.

What additional options for response were there? Teachers who have read the case made the following suggestions: (1) invite the parent to class, (2) send copies of the essays to the parent, and (3) quote documents (such as the California curricular frameworks or Goals 2000) that talk about the need for innovative teaching strategies like groupwork and their benefits. What are the advantages and the disadvantages of these options? Of your proposed response?

Have you ever had experiences like this? What did you do? Have parents criticized groupwork in your class? Have students?

The experience factor

Is the fact that the teacher is new significant to this case? What might be the consequences of the experience for this new teacher? How are her hesitations and vacillations reflected in her narrative? Would veteran teachers have reacted similarly or differently?

Case 15

Walking the Talk: Cooperative Learning for Teachers

Unlike the other cases in *Groupwork in Diverse Classrooms*, which take place in K–12 classrooms, this account focuses on what can happen when *teachers* are assigned to work together in small groups at an inservice workshop. But like many of the K–12 cases, one group experienced numerous problems and made an uneven, disjointed presentation to the larger group. The teacher–author vividly describes what happened in the group, his frustration at being dismissed when he tried to resolve the group's problems, and his anger at professional developers who don't incorporate cooperative learning skills and status treatments into their training sessions.

CONTEXT

The author of this case is a student teacher of mathematics in the Stanford Teacher Education Program. The case takes place at an in-service workshop for an innovative math program which relies heavily on constructive uses of groupwork. When he attended this workshop, the teacher–author was also enrolled in a course on groupwork. The course emphasized the importance of a person's ability to contribute to group tasks, and provided strategies for treating unequal status among group members.

QUESTIONS AND ISSUES

What did this teacher hope to accomplish during this in-service workshop? (Probe for the response that he was testing his ability to apply what he learned in his groupwork course to this in-service workshop.) What do you think he expected would happen? What actually happened? What do you think the staff developers' aspirations were for this in-service session?

What do we know about the group members?

This teacher gives his impression about each of the four group members early in the narrative. How does he describe them? (Probe particularly for language used to describe Dotty.) Based on these descriptions, how do you think the teacher feels about each of the members in his group? How does the fact that Dotty is the only person in the group who had not yet taught the new curriculum put her at a disadvantage for this task?

Examining the task

The teacher said the task for this session differed from those in previous sessions. Previously teachers were given the outline of a unit. They watched how instructors modeled the activities and were then put in groups of four to work through the unit as if they were students. Since they are adults, the instructors assumed they knew how to work harmoniously and never made groupwork an agenda item. Clearly this teacher thought the assumption was faulty. Do you agree?

Look closely at how the teacher described this session's task. What was each group expected to do? How did the task differ from previous sessions?

Pressure point

When the group came together to see if they agreed on their individual products, the teacher said they "didn't get off to the best start." What actually happened? Look specifically at what Dotty said and did. Imagine you were Dotty. How would you have felt when you presented your work and were dismissed by the rest of the group? Put yourself in the place of the others in the group. How would you have reacted to Dotty's presentation? When the teacher asked Dotty what she thought was wrong with the group, Jerry gestured for him to stop talking to her. What would you have done if you were the teacher? If you were Jerry?

After Dotty walked away, the group realized that time was running out and they had not yet prepared their presentation. Without attending to Dotty, they tried to get back to the task at hand. When she returned, Bob and the teacher wanted to address her problem, but Jerry wanted only to get the project done. Look at the text. What did Bob actually say to the teacher? What might the teacher have done if Jerry hadn't stopped him? Evaluate these strategies. Given that the group had to plan a presentation in a short amount of time, would it have been appropriate for the teacher to have intervened and tried to "fix" the problem? Give a rationale for each of your conjectures.

Status problems

The teacher points to status problems as the reason for the group's failure to work together. What was the teacher's perception of the status hierarchy in this group? (Probe for the response that based on his knowledge of mathematics, Jerry was the most sophisticated, and the teacher next best, followed by Bob and Dotty.) Another possibility for attributing status is in terms of teaching experience, in which case the teacher–author might be at the bottom. An additional means of determining status is knowledge of group process, in which case the teacher feels that his knowledge is equal to Jerry's. Dotty probably has low status no matter how you view the situation. If her content knowledge is poor, as the teacher maintains, and she has never taught this particular curriculum, she is at a disadvantage in terms of the group's assignment. What could you do to raise her status in the eyes of other group members?

A plan of action

Given that content knowledge *and* pedagogical content knowledge are needed to accomplish this task, and that Bob and Dotty are weaker in these areas, how might you organize responsibilities for the task if you were a member of this group? What are the risks, benefits, and consequences for each strategy?

Professional development

The teacher felt strongly that the instructors should have included strategies for group process in their in-service seminars, especially since the new mathematics program they were learning relied heavily on groupwork. Do you agree? If so, why? (Probe for the response that there is a need for models of how to prepare and maintain constructive groups in the new

mathematics program.) What would you include if you were a staff developer?

Principles of teaching and learning

Based on this discussion and previous discussions and on your own experience, what principles of teaching and learning in collaborative small groups apply to both children and adults? What principles of staff development are important?

Case 16

We're All in This Together

The third chapter of *Groupwork in Diverse Classrooms* is "One Teacher's Odyssey." Like Odysseus, who undergoes many trials and gains wisdom on his long journey home, the teacher in this case encounters challenges as she becomes an accomplished Complex Instruction teacher (see the casebook introduction for a description of this approach to groupwork). This extended case describes in rich detail a full year of one teacher's groupwork instruction; thus we see a well-rounded depiction of groupwork. The case explores the successes and failures of groupwork and its benefits and costs. It affords opportunities to discuss virtually every dilemma of groupwork.

CONTEXT

The case describes a seventh grade core (combined language arts and social studies) class at a middle school in a semi-rural town which is growing swiftly with the development of rapid transit and new housing. The students are 60% Caucasian, 15% Hispanic, 13% Asian American, and 12% African American. The teacher has taught middle school for 18 years and is a recognized expert in Complex Instruction. In this case she describes and reflects upon her first year using this approach to groupwork.

QUESTIONS AND ISSUES

This case spans a full year, and therefore several units of instruction. In leading a case discussion, we suggest you invite comparisons across the different units and points in the teacher's year. We have structured the discussion topics to move from a focus on the students' varied experiences with groupwork to a focus on the teacher and her growth throughout the year and finally to some common dilemmas of groupwork.

The teacher's role

Several times in the case narrative the teacher reflects upon how Complex Instruction has helped her redefine her role in the classroom. She begins with a description of why teaching appealed to her early in her career.

What does she say about the initial appeal of teaching? How does she describe her changing role? Cite specific incidents or moments that make her aware of her changing role. What aspects of her new role seem to provoke an internal struggle? How do you interpret her struggles? In what ways, if any, does she seem ambivalent about her new role? About Complex Instruction?

In the concluding scene, Ms. Knight poignantly describes Christi sobbing and longing to be part of the group. She says, "I felt both exhilarated and sad. Whatever had happened to Christi had happened to me as well." How do you interpret her closing remarks?

Purposes for groupwork

Throughout the case the teacher examines and evaluates her rationale for groupwork. Prior to her involvement with Complex Instruction, how does she justify her inclusion of groupwork? What are some of her disappointments with groupwork? Despite these disappointments, why does she continue to explore a "way to make it better"?

During the poetry unit, the teacher expresses her doubts about groupwork and whether it is "worth it." How does she allay her doubts?

Where does groupwork fit into the overall scheme of her classroom? What are the variety of groupwork lessons employed? How does the "regular classwork" articulate with the Complex Instruction units? What are the benefits and risks of her approach to groupwork?

The groupwork task

This teacher's notion of a groupwork task derives from specific design criteria used in the construction of Complex Instruction units (i.e., the tasks tap multiple intellectual abilities, are multidimensional, and are open-ended). These criteria are central to productive groupwork because they set the stage for enhanced student access to content, and more important, for students' interdependence. (See the casebook introduction for a more extended discussion of groupwork tasks.)

How does Ms. Knight compare her groupwork tasks before and after Complex Instruction is introduced? What influence do "learning about multiple abilities" appear to have on this teacher's notion of a groupwork task? Reread her descriptions of various tasks, looking for clues that describe the "multiple abilities" necessary to complete them. How do students seem to respond to the inclusion of "multiple abilities"?

Designing tasks so that there is open-endedness and uncertainty ensures students will need each other to complete a task. How do they handle the uncertainty in the poetry unit, which was their first experience with Complex Instruction? In the "Papal bull" incident, their last Complex Instruction unit? How do you explain the different responses to uncertainty in the task? What evidence is there for how the teacher handles assessment of groupwork? (Probe for a mention of a grade for participation, group presentations, etc.) One of the dilemmas of assessment in groupwork is striking a balance between evaluation of the content and/or material students learn and the process the group uses to accomplish its task. In your opinion, how should one assess the individual? The group?

Christi

Christi is the central student in this narrative. How does Ms. Knight introduce her to us? (Probe for examples, e.g., her desire to be a teacher, how she enjoys authority, her organizing, her being expert, how she reminds her of herself as a seventh grader.) Students like Christi are often described as "individualists." What qualities in her character and actions support this description? How does the teacher appear to feel about Christi? How do you think Christi feels about Ms. Knight? Can you think of "Christis" you have had in your classroom? How have you responded to them?

Prior to the introduction of Complex Instruction, what is Christi's typical role in groupwork? How does her role change as Complex Instruction is implemented? The teacher uses the metaphor of "having a rug pulled out from under Christi's sense of security" to describe Christi's reaction to "interdependence." Why do you think Christi responds in this way? What advice would you offer Ms. Knight to help Christi feel more secure?

During the first day of the poetry unit, why does Christi grow impatient with Roberto? Why might Christi react as she does? How do you think the others in the group, especially Roberto, feel? (Probes for a more complete discussion of Roberto appear in the next section.) How does Ms. Knight handle Christi's impatience and the controversy that emerges? What do you think Christi learned in this lesson? How does the episode describing Christi as the dance commissioner enrich our understanding of her?

As the year progresses, Christi's inability to function in groupwork becomes increasingly more aberrant, more "extreme." How do you account for her increasing tantrums and her inability to adapt to this groupwork model? How do you think the other students reacted to her? In what other ways might Ms. Knight have helped Christi cope and adapt?

Roberto

Roberto offers plentiful contrasts to Christi. How does the teacher describe him? Students like Roberto are often characterized as "low-status." What qualities in his character and actions support this description? (Probe for these responses: pushes back desk, shrugs shoulders, smiles, recently left bilingual classroom, barely suppresses his interest.) How does the teacher appear to feel about Roberto? How do you think Roberto feels about Ms. Knight? The others in his class? Can you think of "Robertos" you have had in your classroom? How have you responded to them?

During the first day of the poetry unit, why do the students harangue Roberto? How do you think Roberto felt before and after Ms. Knight stepped in? What do you think Roberto learned in this lesson? Unlike Christi, who fights groupwork with tantrums, Roberto seems to embrace groupwork. How does the teacher describe changes in his classroom behavior? How do you explain these changes? In what ways does Miguel serve as a foil to Roberto?

Ms. Knight says that Roberto spoke up more; she was then able to "point out the value of his contributions," and as a result, "others in the class began to take his opinions more seriously." For sociologists, this is called "assigning competence." This is a strategy designed to change others' perceptions of a low-status person (e.g., change the class's perception of Roberto). By changing others' perceptions of someone, we simultaneously alter others' expectations of what that person can do. Thus when an assignment of competence is successful, others expect the low-status student to be able to contribute or accomplish more than they had before the assignment. In the best of all possible worlds, this change in expectations becomes a self-fulfilling prophecy, with the result that the low-status student participates more meaningfully and eventually learns more.

Let's assess Ms. Knight's assignments of competence. She pointed out the value of Roberto's contributions so others would take him seriously. Why might such an action have an impact on other students? How do you think Roberto felt when he was publicly singled out in this way? What role does a teacher's having noted his abilities play in Roberto's change from a failing student to a passing student? How else might one explain his improved grades? What evidence is there in the text that Ms. Knight's assignment of competence is successful? That it is not successful? How do you interpret Roberto's remark during the Children's Crusade unit that "Before my group complained when I didn't talk, and now they complain when I do"? During the unit on feudal Japan, why do you think Christi and Eddy ignore

Roberto's suggestions for designing a castle? If the teacher's assignment of competence has not been successful, how do you account for that?

Eddy, Eric, Desiree, Leo, and Cyndi

Near the end of the case the teacher introduces a series of students who have differing experiences with groupwork. Why does she introduce them at this point? Review the details of each student's story. In what way is each student unique? In what way is each representative of a type of student? When taken together, what impact do they have upon the case? In conversations with Ms. Knight, she remarked that she saw her class as a "system." How do the descriptions of these other students reflect that view?

Resolving conflicts

The teacher mentions several episodes when she steps in to resolve conflicts. How does she help students overcome an impasse? Resolve their conflicts? In your analysis, how helpful are her interventions? To what extent do strategies for conflict resolution need to be part of the repertoire of a teacher who uses groupwork? How does she appear to decide when she needs to intervene and when students are having a "healthy debate"? Can you suggest additional strategies you would have considered had you been in Ms. Knight's situation?

How might Ms. Knight's approaches to conflict resolution have helped the English teacher in Case 7, "Puzzles of a Well-Crafted Group"?

Picking up the lingo

The teacher remarks at one point that the students have "picked up the lingo pretty well." She goes on to recount a conversation in which the students parrot the reasons for groupwork. How do you interpret the teacher's use of the word "lingo"? Based on your experience, have you encountered students who can state, yet not understand, why they ought to do groupwork, or how they ought to behave during groupwork? How do you respond to them when this happens? Of what value is lingo in teaching kids to work in groups? What are the risks and benefits of introducing lingo?

Composing groups

Unlike many of the teachers in the other cases, this teacher seems almost cavalier about how she composes groups. Why do you think she adopts this attitude toward grouping? What effect might her grouping strategies have on her classroom?

One teacher's odyssey?

What is the significance of the case title? In what sense has Ms. Knight's year been an "odyssey"? What wisdom do you think she has gained as a result of her struggles with groupwork?